100 DAYS

THE GLORY EXPERIMENT

ANGELA SANDERS

LifeWay Press® Nashville, Tennessee

STUDENT MINISTRY PUBLISHING

Ben Trueblood
Director, Student Ministry

John Paul Basham
Manager, Student Ministry Publishing

Karen Daniel
Editorial Team Leader

Stephanie Livengood
Content Editor

Morgan Hawk
Production Editor

Sarah Nikolai
Graphic Designer

ISBN: 978-1-4627-9942-8
Item Number: 005802879

Dewey Decimal Classification Number: 242.2
Subject Heading: DEVOTIONAL LITERATURE/ BIBLE STUDY AND TEACHING / GOD

Printed in the United States of America.

Student Ministry Publishing
LifeWay Resources
One LifeWay Plaza
Nashville, TN 37234-0144

We believe that the Bible has God for its author; salvation for its end; and truth, without any mixture of error, for its matter and that all Scripture is totally true and trustworthy. To review LifeWay's doctrinal guideline, please visit www.lifeway.com/doctrinalguideline.

Unless otherwise noted, all Scripture quotations are taken from the Christian Standard Bible®, Copyright © 2017 by Holman Bible Publishers. Used by permission. Christian Standard Bible® and CSB® are federally registered trademarks of Holman Bible Publishers.

TABLE OF CONTENTS

ABOUT THE AUTHOR

ANGELA SANDERS is a Christian curriculum developer, blogger, and speaker who has a knack for communicating truth in a way everyone can understand. Passionate about God's Word and His church, Angela is grateful for every opportunity to encourage and equip her brothers and sisters in Christ. She has ghost-written over 2,000 widely distributed daily personal Bible study guides published by the Baptist General Convention of Oklahoma and other ministry entities, as well as group Bible studies, ministry manuals, and over 400 journalistic profiles. Angela's articles, stories, and dramas have appeared in various Christian magazines, and her blog draws a regular following. Angela and her husband, Todd, have been married for 25 years. They and their two children, Hunter and Hope, make their home in Edmond, Oklahoma. You can follow Angela on Twitter and Instagram @aswrites and visit her website at www.angelasanderswrites.com.

WHY 100 DAYS?

100 Days: The Glory Experiment was written in direct response to a perceived need in the church to reclaim lost ground in the area of discipleship. This Bible study and all-in-one discipleship guide seeks to strengthen the church by building up individuals who build up one another.

This study challenges users to glorify God in their attitudes, words, actions, and reactions for at least 100 days and to invite others to join them.

100 Days makes it easy for Christians of all ages and spiritual maturity levels to go and make disciples (on their own or through their churches), while continuously pointing believers back to the body of Christ for support, encouragement, and accountability.

Throughout the study, you will be encouraged to begin, maintain, and multiply *100 Days* groups and will be told exactly how to do so. These groups will be more for discussion than content delivery. The Discipleship Group Guide provided in this book contains questions that apply to all sections within the study, making it possible for new members to jump in and participate at any point in the life of a *100 Days* group.

Why *100 Days*? Because there's nothing else like it.

BEFORE YOU BEGIN

So, whether you eat or drink, or whatever you do, do everything for the glory of God. —1 Corinthians 10:31

Glory. It's a church word if there ever was one. Your parents use it. Your grandparents use it. We all sing about it in church, but what does it mean?

Glory is honor bestowed on anything that inspires admiration. God's glory is His divine perfection, any display of His divine perfection, or praise and worship offered in response to His divine perfection.

To glorify is to hold up for admiration or to honor with praise and worship. To glorify God is to hold up for admiration His divine perfection, any display of His divine perfection, or to praise and worship Him in response to who He is and what He's done.

God is all about His glory, and rightly so. Considering who He is and what He has done for us, we should be too.

CONDUCTING THE EXPERIMENT

- Consider The Question.
- Consider taking The Challenge.
- Complete all 100 devotions on your own, developing a deeper relationship with God. When you reach the end of those 100 days, you will be able to answer The Question.
- Catch The Vision and pass it on.

THE QUESTION

What would happen if you lived 100 days for God's glory alone?

The only way to find out is to just do it.

THE CHALLENGE

Consider taking this challenge:

> I commit to make a full and conscious effort to glorify God through my attitude, words, actions, and reactions for at least 100 days.

Signed: _____

Date: _____

To help you stay strong and finish *The Glory Experiment*, consider taking an extra step:

> I will choose three people to hold me accountable to this commitment by praying for me, asking me to share what I'm learning through *100 Days*, encouraging me to persevere until the 100 days are complete (even when I want to give up), and correcting me with patience and in love when my attitude, words, actions, or reactions don't glorify God.

These people will hold me accountable:

Signed: _____

Signed: _____

Signed: _____

THE VISION

The Vision is viral discipleship.

When you complete *The Glory Experiment*, you will be encouraged to retake The Challenge and with your current group or pass on what you've learned to others. The key is to live for God's glory even after you have answered the questions on these pages.

100 Days groups are designed to continue meeting even after individual members have moved on and should create new groups as they grow—disciples making disciples.

Viral discipleship is possible. You just have to take the first step and let the Holy Spirit take it from there.

ON YOUR OWN

Spend a small part of each day studying your Bible and the rest thinking about and doing what it says. To get the very most out of *The Glory Experiment*, do the following:

- Grab your Bible or download the CSB app on your phone.
- Keep your thoughts focused on God and live each day for His glory.
- Work through the daily devotions in order, at your own pace. Some may take you more than one day, but that's okay. It's more important to complete all the devotions than it is to finish the experiment in exactly 100 days. Take your time when studying so you can fully understand and apply what you read. The goal is daily consistency, not speed. Just keep at it.
- As you work your way through this devotional, jot down any questions you have under As You Go at the beginning of each chapter. Ask God to answer your questions in His timing.
- If you want to invite friends to join you at any point during *The Glory Experiment*, go ahead! The *100 Days* group questions in the Discipleship Group Guide (pp. 212-217) apply to all the individual devotions. You don't have to keep pace with one another to talk about what God is teaching you, so it should be easy for your friends to jump in anytime. Just don't take members from an existing *100 Days* group unless given the okay to do so by their group leader. Find people who aren't already involved in a group instead.
- When you complete *100 Days: The Glory Experiment*, fill out the evaluation in The End? (pp. 209-211). Consider taking The Challenge and working through the devotions again to see what else God has to say to you. You may want to lead a small group the next time through. If you've already led one, you can either keep leading the same group or start a new one.

CHAPTER ONE

THE GOSPEL

**What does it look like to glorify God
in my response to the gospel?**

AS YOU GO

Sometimes serious Bible study raises more questions than it answers. That's okay! Spiritual growth is a process. As you work your way through Chapter 1, you can record your questions on this page.

When God gives you the answers, write them down. Don't worry if it takes a while. Remember, God promises to be found by those who seek Him (Jer. 29:13), and He always keeps His promises (2 Cor. 1:20).

QUESTION	ANSWER	SCRIPTURAL PROOF

GOD'S ROLE IN THE GOSPEL

We all like to receive good news, and we're about to dig into the best good news: the gospel of Jesus Christ. The gospel of Jesus Christ is found in the Bible. The Bible is the Word of God, written down by men (2 Tim. 3:16; 2 Pet. 1:21).

No matter your current feelings toward, beliefs about, or relationship with God, becoming familiar with the gospel and God's Word is a good first step toward learning what it means to glorify God. Then, you can decide for yourself whether or not that's what you really want to do with your life.

Jump to The Truth section in the back of this book. Read the About God list on page 218. Place a check mark by the truths that are easy for you to believe. Place a question mark by the truths that are difficult for you to believe.

Now, look back at the marks you made. Why do you struggle to believe the truths with question marks by them?

READ HEBREWS 11:1,6.

FOLLOWERS OF CHRIST;
LITERALLY MEANS "LITTLE CHRISTS"

These verses are part of a letter written to encourage early Hebrew Christians. Although the Hebrew Christians had put their faith in Jesus Christ for salvation, some of them struggled to live out that faith with confidence because their neighbors didn't believe in the gospel of Jesus Christ.

In what ways do you relate to the early Hebrew Christians?

READ EPHESIANS 2:8-9.

A GROUP OF CHRISTIANS

These verses are part of a letter the apostle Paul wrote to the early church in Ephesus. It was a circular letter, meaning it was supposed to be passed around from church to church. This letter contained doctrine Paul believed every Christian should know and embrace.

Where does faith come from according to this passage?

Belief and faith are two very different things. Believing in something is agreeing that it's real or true. Having faith in something requires not only believing in it, but also trusting it to bring about promised results and living according to that trust. True faith leads to action.

Many people claim to have faith in God, but only those who respond appropriately to the gospel of Jesus Christ actually do. An appropriate response includes accepting God's forgiveness for sin and surrendering our lives to follow Jesus in obedience.

Using the definitions given above, do you believe in God? Why or why not?

Have you put your faith in Him? Explain.

How does the faith you show glorify God? How does it do the opposite at times?

What God taught me today and what I plan to do about it:

_____

_____

_____

_____

_____

_____

JESUS' ROLE IN THE GOSPEL

Jesus may be the most misunderstood figure in human history. Rumors about who He is, why He came, and what really happened to Him 2,000 years ago are still circulating. Today, you'll get the truth.

Turn to The Truth section of this book. Read the About Jesus list on page 219. Place a check mark by the truths that are easy for you to believe. Place a question mark by the truths that are difficult for you to believe.

Review the marks you made. Why do you struggle to believe the truths with question marks by them?

READ MATTHEW 7:7-11,28-29.

The Books of Matthew, Mark, Luke, and John are collectively known as the Gospels because they focus on Jesus' life and teaching. Each book is named after its author.

This passage is part of the Sermon on the Mount, which Jesus preached to a crowd of people who followed Him all over Galilee as He taught and healed the sick. Matthew and Jesus' other disciples were part of that crowd. What Jesus taught went against the way many of them had been thinking and living. The crowd struggled to take it all in, since it was so different from what the scribes taught. Believing what Jesus said and following Him would require great faith on their part, faith they couldn't possibly build up on their own.

In what ways can you relate to Jesus' audience? What about the disciples specifically?

What do you need from God today that would help strengthen your faith?

How does asking God for what you need glorify Him?

What God taught me today and what I plan to do about it:

_____

_____

_____

_____

_____

_____

_____

_____

_____

_____

_____

_____

_____

_____

_____

_____

_____

_____

YOUR ROLE IN THE GOSPEL

The truth hurts sometimes, but it always sets you free (John 8:32). Whether today's truth is new to you or all too familiar, open your heart and let God's truth do its work.

Check out the About Us list on page 221 in The Truth section of this book. Place a check mark by the truths that are easy for you to believe. Place a question mark by the truths that are difficult for you to believe.

Go through the marks you made. Why do you struggle to believe the truths with question marks by them?

READ ROMANS 3:23; 5:12.

These two verses are a part of what some call the Roman Road to Salvation. This "road" was a part of Paul's letter to the church in Rome, in which he explained in simple terms what it takes to become a Christian.

Highlight the words "all have sinned" in your Bible. As you complete this study, keep in mind that sin is anything that goes against God's will or nature.

What effect do these verses have on you?

READ ROMANS 6:23.

Break down the verse into the following:

Difficult Truth	Good News

READ ROMANS 5:8.

What stands out to you in this verse? Why?

READ ROMANS 10:9-10,13.

What do we have to do to be saved from the consequences
of sin according to these verses?

Have you done this? If so, describe that experience. How has it changed your
life? How has it glorified God? If not, what might be holding you back from
making the decision to follow Jesus?

From beginning to end, salvation is the work of God, a gift. He makes us aware of
our sin (Rom. 3:20). He convicts, or convinces, us of that sin and draws our hearts
toward repentance (John 6:44-45; 16:8), and He gives us the faith to believe.
Even so, it's our job to apply that faith by choosing to follow Jesus. It's our job to
surrender. Only when we do that will we be saved from the consequences of sin
and become children of God.

If you want to know more about trusting in Jesus as your Savior, check out
So You've Been Introduced to Jesus. Now What? on page 211 of this study.

What God taught me today and what I plan to do about it:

_____

_____

_____

_____

ONE WAY TO GOD

God's plan of salvation is simple—so simple that some people struggle to believe it. They just don't see how putting their faith in Jesus could possibly be enough to cover sin as great as theirs, but it is. Jesus is always enough.

READ JOHN 14:6.

Jesus spoke these words to His disciples. He knew they would have to defend and explain the gospel after He'd gone back to heaven, especially to those who preached a different or additional way to get to God.

What is the only way to be **reconciled** to God? | BROUGHT BACK INTO RIGHT RELATIONSHIP WITH GOD |

What are some ways people often try to make things right with God aside from placing their faith in Jesus? How does this demonstrate a lack of faith? Explain.

READ GALATIANS 1:3-9; 3:1-5.

Even though they'd been spared the consequences of sin through faith in Jesus, the new believers in Galatia still had trouble believing that a gift as wonderful as salvation could be so simple.

When others stepped in and told them they needed to do something more to be saved, the Galatian Christians fell for it and started trying to earn their salvation— something that can't possibly be done. Because he loved them and wanted to see God glorified, Paul set them straight.

On what or whom do you rely day in and day out for your salvation? How do your words and actions demonstrate what or who you rely on?

What actions might demonstrate a life of faith? How does this glorify God?

What actions might indicate someone is not a Christian?

Think about the way you answered the previous questions. Does your life glorify God?

What God taught me today and what I plan to do about it:

THE GOSPEL AND THE HOLY SPIRIT

Salvation is not the end of your spiritual journey. It's only the beginning.

Read the About the Holy Spirit list in the back of this book on page 220. Place a check mark by the ones you have experienced personally.

Which of these truths do you find encouraging? Why?

READ GALATIANS 4:6-7.

Slaves don't inherit their master's kingdom; sons and daughters do. When we put our faith in Jesus Christ, the Holy Spirit comes to dwell within us. His presence not only guarantees that we are permanently adopted children of God, but also ensures that we inherit God's kingdom right along with Jesus, our brother.

Has God sent the Holy Spirit into your heart? How do you know?

What does this say about your relationship to God?

Why do you think God chose to display His glory by sending the Holy Spirit to live in flawed human beings?

Your position as heir to God's kingdom ensures that your eternity is secure and you'll never want for anything on a spiritual level. It's all been provided by God, your freedom, your peace, your joy, and your blessings. This fact should give you confidence, inspire gratitude, and change the way you handle difficulties while you're still here on earth.

How should knowing you have a big inheritance coming affect the way you handle yourself now? How will your behavior glorify God?

READ PHILIPPIANS 2:12-13.

These verses are from a letter the apostle Paul wrote to the church in Philippi. It may sound like Paul was telling the Philippian Christians they had to earn their own salvation, but that's not true. He was encouraging them not to take their relationship with God for granted, but to work to understand what God wanted them to do with the salvation He gave them.

What encouragement do you find in these verses? What challenge?

According to this passage, is there any good excuse for disobeying God? Explain.

Examine your heart. Does your current level of obedience glorify God? Why or why not?

What changes can you make in your life to choose obedience more often?

What God taught me today and what I plan to do about it:

_____

_____

_____

_____

GOD'S ULTIMATE GOAL

God's ultimate purpose in sending His Son, Jesus, to rescue us had more to do with His own glory than it had to do with us. No matter how much we want to believe we're worth the sacrifice God made, it's just not true. Our worth is a direct result of our being created and then rescued by a perfect God. We're only worth something because He's worth everything.

READ EPHESIANS 1:11-14.

God made a way for us to be saved through Jesus Christ, and He gives the Holy Spirit to those who put their faith in Jesus for salvation. He does this so people will recognize His perfection and praise Him for it—the same reason He does everything else. And why not? He *is* God. Such behavior might be considered prideful or arrogant if we did it, but that's because we're flawed. God alone is perfect, and His glory deserves recognition and praise.

How do human arrogance and pride keep us from giving God the amount of praise and recognition He deserves?

How does hero worship interfere with God's receiving the recognition and praise He deserves?

Are you giving God the recognition and praise He deserves? Are you glorifying Him? Why or why not?

READ EPHESIANS 2:4-7.

Just to be clear, to love others is to serve others. To show grace is to treat others better than they deserve to be treated. To show mercy is to show kind and compassionate restraint when dealing with those who've done something wrong. To show kindness is to give without promise of reciprocation or gain.

Describe the ways God has shown you each of the following:

Love:

Grace:

Mercy:

Kindness:

Does the way you respond to God's love, grace, mercy, and kindness glorify Him? Explain.

What God taught me today and what I plan to do about it:

_____

_____

_____

_____

_____

_____

_____

_____

JESUS' ULTIMATE GOAL

Although He loves us, Jesus' death on the cross had more to do with His commitment to obey God and serve God's ultimate purpose than it had to do with any emotion or obligation He felt toward us.

READ MARK 14:32-36.

This is part of a prayer Jesus prayed in the Garden of Gethsemane the night He was arrested, just a few days before He was crucified on the cross.

Jesus loves us. He proved it in countless ways during His ministry here on earth. However, Jesus still asked if there was any other way for God to rescue us. Like anyone else would, Jesus probably wanted to avoid the excruciating agony of the cross. But this doesn't lessen the nobility of His sacrifice. If anything, it makes His choice to follow through in obedience even more meaningful and takes away any excuse we might offer God for not doing the same.

READ JOHN 17:4-5.

This passage comes from a prayer Jesus prayed out loud for the benefit of those listening and our benefit too (John 17:13). In this prayer, Jesus references His own crucifixion and prays for those who would later follow Him in obedience.

According to this passage, what was Jesus' ultimate goal in life? In death?

How does it line up with God's goal in sending Him to rescue us?

In what way did Jesus' obedience glorify God? What did it prove? To whom?

READ PHILIPPIANS 2:5-11.

Describe how God rewarded Jesus' obedience.

How was God glorified in His own response to Jesus' obedience? What did His response prove?

What God taught me today and what I plan to do about it:

_____

_____

_____

_____

_____

_____

_____

_____

_____

_____

_____

_____

_____

_____

YOUR ULTIMATE GOAL

Salvation is a free gift to us; there is nothing we can do to earn it. God did not give us this gift and expect us to live up to some impossible standard. He does not require works from us in exchange for our salvation. He knows we will struggle with sin, and we will sometimes fall into disobedience. That's where His grace comes in. However, this is not a license to sin. The way we respond to God's gracious gift of salvation should be evident in our lives.

One of the ways our salvation is most evident is in the way we seek to live our lives in line with God's will and Word. As we are refined and sanctified through our relationship with Him, we should increasingly want to please Him—exchanging our will, desires, and goals for His. We obey out of love and gratitude for what God has done for us, not because we *have* to, but because we *want* to.

READ 1 CORINTHIANS 10:31.

This verse is part of a letter Paul wrote to the early church in Corinth. The Corinthian believers struggled to live for God while being surrounded by people who were living for themselves. In a city known for its wickedness, Paul encouraged the Corinthian believers to make God known in all they did.

What should be the ultimate goal of every Christian?

Obey Jesus out of love.

Looking back at previous devotions, does this match Jesus' goal? Does it match God's? Explain.

What portion of a Christian's life should be devoted to achieving this goal?

all of it — because when we follow the Lord wholeheartedly we can do the best Kingdom Work

In what ways does the situation the Corinthians faced seem similar to many of the situations you face today? → friendgroup
being in highschool.

How will making God's glory your ultimate goal impact the way you make decisions and interact with people?
when everything His glory we lean into him in that and he gaives Jus the ability to pour into people well & fruits of the spirit

What are some differences this might make in your prayer life?
thanking God for the little things.

How will it glorify God?
→ when God helps me find JOY in the little things I will be able to see him everywher (BIG and small) and doing kingdom work won't feel like something I have to do but something I want to do.

What God taught me today and what I plan to do about it:

_____

_____

_____

_____

_____

_____

_____

_____

_____

_____

_____

_____

DAY 9

JESUS' MISSION, OUR MISSION

No matter the obstacle, temptation, or potential distraction, Jesus never lost sight of His mission or the ultimate purpose behind it. As His followers, neither should we.

READ LUKE 19:2-10 AND PHILIPPIANS 2:5-8.

People were no less opinionated in Jesus' day than they are now, but Jesus didn't care what they thought. Jesus' mission and main focus was glorifying God by completing the mission God had given Him. Jesus obeyed the Father even when it made Him unpopular.

What was Jesus' mission?

To seek and save the lost

What did He do to achieve it? Revisit the About Jesus list on page 219 for help if you need to.

He pursued the people who were the most difficult. He loved people where they are at.

What are some ways Jesus' obedience affects you personally?

READ ROMANS 10:14-15.

If you don't know something is available, you can't do anything about it. That's why it's so important for all Christians to do their part to spread the gospel. If all of us go to the people God intends for us to reach and say what God intends for us to say, no one will have an excuse for not responding appropriately to the gospel. Everyone will have a chance to trust Jesus as Savior!

Have you ever shared the gospel with someone? Describe that experience.

yes, every tuesday at groups, when people ask me what I want to be when I'm older

How does your obedience in sharing the gospel glorify God?

KINGDOM WORK → we are called to make disciples of the nations

If you haven't shared the gospel with someone, what's holding you back?

Make no mistake, God doesn't need you to spread the gospel—He's more than capable of accomplishing His purposes with or without you. God lets you spread the gospel, so you can fully understand what's yours through Jesus Christ (Philem. 1:6) and share His joy when someone is saved. If you don't, you're missing out!

What God taught me today and what I plan to do about it:

→ All GLORY FOR THE KINGDOM
→ eyes fixed on Jesus

knowing these things sharing my faith with people won't be a chore because when your eyes are fixed on Jesus it happens naturally.

YOUR RESPONSIBILITY

TELLING OTHERS ABOUT JESUS

Some people think evangelism is a job for ministers and missionaries—and they're right. If you are a Christian, you are a missionary and a minister. All believers have been called by God to join Jesus on His mission to seek and save the lost and to serve as ministers of reconciliation by taking God's message of reconciliation to the world.

READ 2 CORINTHIANS 5:17-20.

This passage comes from Paul's second letter to the church at Corinth. Apparently, Paul's first letter wasn't received well. Some false teachers made their way to Corinth, and it seems that they convinced the believers to turn their backs on Paul and the gospel he preached. Some time after this, Paul wrote a letter rebuking the Corinthian believers. Timothy then reported to Paul that the majority of the believers had repented. Relieved by the change, Paul wrote this letter to refocus the church on their mission.

According to this passage, when God calls us to salvation, He also calls us to evangelism. In other words, the moment we trust in Jesus for salvation, we become responsible for sharing the gospel with other people.

What might lead new Christians to think they should wait before telling others about Jesus?

I think personal hesitation because some may feel unfit.

What can they do to overcome those misconceptions or obstacles?

pray, dig into the fact that Jesus redeems the most broken.

READ 1 CORINTHIANS 2:3-5. *↳ look at who Jesus pursued.*

The church in Corinth had a hard time gaining traction in a culture conditioned to resist the message of the gospel. In this passage, Paul reminded the church members of his own limitations and God's power to work in spite of our flaws.

Which means more to you, seeing people saved or preserving your self-image? What evidence can you give to support your answer? *seeing people saved ↝ everything we do should for the kingdom.*

According to this passage, does a Christian have to be a polished communicator to share the good news of Jesus Christ with others? Why or why not? *no, the HOLY SPIRIT can work through you!*

Who draws people to God? Then, who deserves the glory for their decision? Explain. *We can show people who God is through our actions but God deserves ALL THE GLORY*

> ONE WAY TO INTRODUCE PEOPLE TO THE GOSPEL IS TO GIVE THEM A COPY OF *100 DAYS: THE GLORY EXPERIMENT* AND INVITE THEM TO JOIN A *100 DAYS* GROUP.

How does your willingness to share the gospel—even when you feel inadequate—glorify God? *shows your faith and trust that he will provide*

What God taught me today and what I plan to do about it:

→ nothing should stop you from sharing the gospel
↳ ALL FOR THE KINGDOM
→ GOD PROVIDES IN OUR WEAKNESS

DAY 11

CREATING OPPORTUNITIES

You've probably heard the saying that people don't care what you know until they know you care. What you know about Jesus Christ has the power to change lives for eternity, so you need to take advantage of every opportunity God gives you to show people how much you care.

READ EPHESIANS 2:10.

What encouragement do you find in this verse? Explain.

Describe the challenge you find in this verse.

READ MATTHEW 5:14-16.

Jesus is the Light of the World (John 8:12). Those of us who have the Holy Spirit in our hearts as a result of our faith in Him have that light inside us. It's our responsibility to shine that light everywhere we go, not to make ourselves look good, but to help others see how good He is.

List some good deeds that you've done lately. Next to each, tell why you did it.

Are your good deeds serving God's purpose? Explain.

READ ROMANS 1:16 AND 1 PETER 3:15-16.

Peter was one of Jesus' apostles. The apostles were a group of twelve men Jesus called out from a larger group of disciples (or students) to follow Him and assist in His ministry. Peter wrote these words to prepare and encourage Christians all over the world. He knew that the gospel message wouldn't always be well received. He also knew that the disciples could be mistreated for their faith, so he encouraged them to take advantage of every opportunity—those created by their good deeds and those created by their suffering—to spread the gospel.

Describe how doing good deeds creates opportunities to share the gospel.

What will you say to people when they ask why you serve others the way you do?

Why is it so important to share the gospel with gentleness and respect?

What might cause a Christian to feel ashamed of the gospel? Is this an appropriate response? Explain.

How will sharing the gospel with confidence glorify God?

What God taught me today and what I plan to do about it:

_____

_____

_____

_____

REVIEW DAY

Take a minute to look back through what you've learned and written throughout this first chapter. Then, answer the following questions:

On a scale of 1 to 10, how much effort have you put into completing your daily Bible study guides?

5 ← not a lot, non nothing

How much attention have you devoted to hearing God's voice? What has He said to you?

→ a lot of attention to His voice
↳ He reassured me that: my identity is in Him & He is greater always

In what ways have you tried to carry out the plans God told you to make? How has God used your obedience?

Keeping my eyes toward Jesus when things aren't going my way.

How has living intentionally for God's glory affected you so far? How has it affected those around you?

Made me have more -JOY- and treat my relation-ships with more grace.

If you aren't part of a *100 Days* group yet, consider starting one of your own! See the Discipleship Group Guide for more instructions.

PRAYER

- Thank God for the Bible and for speaking to your heart.
- Thank Him for loving you and for the privilege of glorifying Him through your obedience.
- Thank Him for any results that may have come from your obedience.
- Make any commitments you need to make going forward and ask God for the desire and ability to follow through on those commitments.

monday motivation: you are not defined by what you've been through, you are defined by God's love for you

CHAPTER TWO

GOD THE FATHER

How can I glorify God in the way I respond to Him?

AS YOU GO

As you work your way through Chapter 2 of this study, you can record your questions here. When God gives you the answers, fill them in.

QUESTION	ANSWER	SCRIPTURAL PROOF

THE TRUTH ABOUT GOD

Take a minute to read through the About God list on page 218. As you read each statement, consider its meaning, weight, and what it has to do with you. Put a star by the ones that stand out to you.

Don't rush through it and take all the time you need to let God's Word sink in.

Now, revisit the truths you checked. Choose the two truths that affect you the most. Write out those truths and answer the questions following each one.

TRUTH 1:

What does this truth have to do with me?

How does God want me to respond? What are some practical steps I can take?

How will my appropriate response glorify God and advance the gospel?

TRUTH 2:

What does this truth have to do with me?

How does God want me to respond? What are some practical steps
I can take?

How will my appropriate response glorify God and advance the gospel?

What God taught me today and what I plan to do about it:

EXPERIENCING AWE

How you choose to respond to the truth about God from now on will tell you a lot about the condition of your heart.

READ PSALM 47:2.

> SONS OF KORAH WERE USUALLY TEMPLE SINGERS AND GATEKEEPERS.

This verse is taken from a song of praise to God written by the descendants of Korah. Korah was a leader among God's chosen people and a part of the temple ministry, but he wasn't content with that assignment. Korah wanted Moses' and Aaron's jobs, so he rebelled against their authority.

These days, the word *awesome* is incredibly overused. We've grown desensitized to its meaning, but the sons of Korah understood it well and spoke from personal experience. To be awesome is to inspire awe. To experience awe is to be amazed to the point of being overwhelmed.

Considering what you know about God now. Would you use the word awesome to describe Him? Explain.

How has God proven Himself to be awesome in your life?

Would you explain your response to God on a daily basis as awe? Why or why not? If not, what changes can you make to live more in awe of God each day?

READ ISAIAH 6:1-7.

Isaiah was a prophet who encouraged God's people to obey God and put their faith in Him instead of putting their faith in other people or what they could accomplish for themselves.

Was the prophet Isaiah's response to God in this passage appropriate? Why or why not?

How does the word *awe* match Isaiah's response?

What was God's response to Isaiah's confession?

Compare your interaction with God so far to Isaiah's interaction with God here. What are the similarities and differences?

How will expressing your awe of God glorify Him and influence your mission?

What God taught me today and what I plan to do about it:

_____

_____

_____

_____

_____

_____

_____

_____

DAY 15

FEARING GOD

Awe inspires humility, but fear inspires obedience.

READ LUKE 12:4-7.

Jesus spoke these words to His disciples well into His ministry on earth. They'd been following Jesus for a while, and many more had begun to flock to Jesus. People were curious and hopeful that He might hold the answers they were looking for after they heard about His revolutionary teaching and the miracles He performed. However, the spiritual leaders of the day were upset by Jesus' growing popularity and started looking for a reason to arrest Him. It was a tumultuous time, to say the least. The disciples felt the tension, no doubt.

At first glance, Jesus seems to be contradicting Himself in these verses. He told His disciples not to be afraid and then turned right around and told them to fear God. A closer look at the connotations, or implied meanings, of these two words clears things up.

Fright, or terror, is an immediate, uncontrollable physical response to real or imagined danger. To be afraid is to live in a continued state of apprehension or dread even after having time to process the validity of the danger. To fear is to honor or worship in reverence and submission, or to hold in such high regard that you serve or obey whatever it is you fear.

Imagine you were one of the disciples listening to Jesus speak these words. How would you have responded?

What or who scares you? Why?

How does your relationship with God help you respond appropriately to what scares you?

When we fear God, we humbly submit (surrender to) His authority in our lives.

How does knowing His place in your life encourage you toward reverence and awe (fear)?

What are some ways your decision to fear God alone will glorify Him?

How will your decision not to be afraid impact your mission?

What God taught me today and what I plan to do about it:

TRUSTING GOD

To fear is to obey. To trust is to rest in and rely on. God is worthy of both your fear and your trust.

READ PROVERBS 3:5-6.

The Book of Proverbs is a compilation of wisdom based on the knowledge of God, written mostly by King Solomon. Solomon knew from personal experience how dangerous it could be to trust in anything other than God. He also knew the benefit of wisdom, the one thing He asked God to give him (1 Chron. 1:8-11).

Worldly wisdom and godly wisdom are not the same, worldly wisdom says to "trust yourself," "go with your gut," or "follow your heart." But Solomon advised us to go the right way—pursue God with everything in you, and He will show you where to go and how to do what He's called you to do.

Record the command given in this passage in your own words.

Is this command an easy or difficult one for you to obey? Explain.

Review the About God list on page 218. What do you find there that would help you obey this command?

What is God's promise to those who obey this command? Why does this matter to someone who wants to glorify God?

READ ROMANS 8:28 AND EPHESIANS 1:11.

Remember, God's ultimate purpose in everything He does is His own glory, and our ultimate purpose in everything we do should also be His glory.

What did God promise in these verses?

Explain how these two verses work together.

God does not promise that all things will be wonderful in our lives all the time or that we will only experience positive life situations and changes. What He does promise is that all of those things—positive or negative—will ultimately work together for our good and His glory.

God is sovereign over all of creation and every circumstance in our lives. He knows what's happening to us, what our struggles are, and what we need. Jesus put it this way: He even knows the number of hairs on your head (Luke 12:6-7,22-34).

What must you value to be able to take comfort in these verses? Explain.

Are you truly trusting God? What evidence can you offer?

Why might failing to trust God under pressure hinder your mission?

How will trusting God in all circumstances glorify Him?

What God taught me today and what I plan to do about it:

_____

_____

_____

APPROACHING GOD

God takes no pleasure in punishing people, but wants them to repent so He can forgive them.

READ EZEKIEL 18:23. | GOD'S CHOSEN PEOPLE |

Throughout the Old Testament, the Jews showed symptoms of the same sin nature we struggle with today. They would serve and obey God for a while—usually right after He had done something amazing for them—and then turn away from Him to chase after other things that seemed to serve their purposes better at the time. During one such rebellious period, God allowed the Jews to be taken as hostages by King Nebuchadnezzar to Babylon to get their attention.

Ezekiel served as prophet to these Jews (Ezek. 1:1). He spent his life reminding them it was their sin that led to their exile, while at the same time reassuring them of God's faithfulness in spite of that sin. He continually encouraged them to love and obey God. Here, Ezekiel passed along a direct quote from God to those in rebellion.

What wrong idea did the Jews have about God?

What evidence have you seen that people still believe this lie today? Explain.

How does this lie hinder the gospel?

Describe the truth God shared with the Jews.

Will telling people the truth about God glorify Him? Why or why not?

READ PSALM 103:8-14.

This passage is from a song of praise written by King David. During his reign, King David committed sin that carried hefty consequences for himself and others. He couldn't hide what he'd done because it was very public. But thanks to God's mercy and grace, David was able to accept God's forgiveness, move past the guilt of bringing disgrace on himself and his family, and live a life of freedom and joy in obedience to God.

List some key differences between David's description of God and the rumors some people spread about Him.

Do you think more people would come to God with their sin and brokenness like David did if they knew the truth about God? Why or why not?

What do David's words tell us about God? How does that affect your view of God?

How will your willingness to approach God with your sin glorify Him and help you accomplish your mission?

What God taught me today and what I plan to do about it:

_____

_____

_____

DAY 18

BEING HONEST WITH GOD

Trying to do for yourself what only God can do is wasted effort—it only wears you out and keeps you from knowing Him as well as you want.

READ PSALM 30:8-12.

Today's passages are taken from two of King David's prayers to God. The first prayer was on the behalf of God's people, Israel.

What did David ask God to do in this prayer?

List the reason(s) David gave for his request.

Summarize God's response to David's request.

What lesson can you learn from David?

At first, David's request seems a little arrogant, but he's not saying that if something bad happened to him and his people no one else would praise God. He knew that wasn't true! He was just letting God know that he fully intended to spend his life praising God if he and his people were spared. David knew God's glory is more important to Him than anything else, so this was a wise thing for David to do.

READ PSALM 51:10-17.

Although King David struggled, the Bible says he was a man after God's own heart (Acts 13:22). He knew where to turn when he messed up, and he didn't pretend to be perfect. Instead, David honestly poured out his heart before God. Like David, we can shake loose sin's hold on our lives and step into the forgiveness God freely offers.

What can you tell about David's attitude toward God in these verses?

What did David want? Why? How does David's desire line up with God's ultimate purpose?

Why do you suppose God considered David to be a man after His own heart? (Hint: Reread Acts 13:22.)

Where should you turn for help when you sin, suspect that your spiritual focus is off, or feel your enthusiasm for God starting to dwindle? How will doing so glorify God?

What God taught me today and what I plan to do about it:

OFFERING GOD PRAISE AND WORSHIP

GIVE HONOR, RESPECT, OR DEVOTION

When you worship something, you serve that thing or person with your life—you think, feel, act, and react in the best interest of whatever it is you worship. Even when you don't realize it and even when you aren't sure what you're worshiping, you're still worshiping something.

Those who worship God serve His glory—acting, thinking, reacting, and feeling in ways that will respect and honor God. Our worship blesses us individually, and our corporate worship blesses others.

BELIEVERS GATHERED TOGETHER TO WORSHIP

READ PSALM 29:2.

To "ascribe to the Lord the glory due His name" is to praise, or compliment, God. It's to give Him the credit, recognition, and honor He deserves for being who He is.

In what ways do your thoughts give God the glory due to Him? In what ways do they need to change?

Do your words, both those you speak to God and those you speak to others, glorify and honor God? Explain.

How do your actions—seen and unseen—glorify and honor God?

In what ways does your attitude toward people and situations glorify and honor God? In what areas does your attitude still need some work? Explain.

The second part of this verse says to "worship the LORD in the splendor of his holiness," which means to respond appropriately to the beauty of His divine perfection. It is to make a point of expressing awe and gratitude in response to who He is and what He has done. You can do this through music, prayer, reading or proclaiming God's Word, serving the church, evangelism, and giving tithes and offerings. Really, any obedient expression of a heart bowed low before God is an act of worship.

Describe your response to God's glory and how you express it.

What do you do in private recognition of God's glory?

What do you do in public recognition of God's glory?

Do you think your worship glorifies Him? Why or why not?

What God taught me today and what I plan to do about it:

_____

_____

_____

_____

_____

_____

_____

_____

SINCERE WORSHIP

There's a big difference between going to church and really worshiping God. We confuse the two sometimes, but God never does.

READ JOHN 4:23-24.

To worship God in spirit and truth is to humble yourself before God and offer your devotion, allegiance, and praise in response to His glory with absolute sincerity.

> GOD COMMANDS US TO PARTICIPATE IN CERTAIN ACTS OF WORSHIP, LIKE BAPTISM AND THE LORD'S SUPPER. THESE ARE CALLED ORDINANCES.

We can worship God in spirit and truth through corporate worship and/or observing biblical ordinances. But words only count as worship if you mean them, and actions only count as worship if they are inspired by God. In other words, we can worship God alongside others, but doing what the Christians around you are doing just to impress or make them happy won't please God.

List some indicators that you're worshiping God in spirit and truth and not just going through the motions.

How will worshiping God in spirit and truth glorify Him?

Sincere worship can be done when you're alone or when you're with other believers. It doesn't matter who's around you, what state you're in, or how many people you serve or sing alongside. Our worship of God is not bound by location, but is defined by the sincerity of our hearts.

READ ISAIAH 29:13-16.

This passage is God's response to the Jews who had been going through the motions of worship without meaning any of what they said or did. Apparently, they thought they could fool God into accepting their half-hearted efforts. They were wrong.

What did God want from the Jews?

What does God want from you?

How are you responding in obedience? If you aren't, what do you need to change in order to respond in obedience?

The Jews failed in their attempts to hide their actions from God. He knew their hearts were sinful and far from Him. Rather than offering their hearts to God for His service, they instead offered "lip-service." In other words, their praise was empty, and God knew it. We can easily get caught in this trap of going through the motions. God knows when our praise is empty and when our hearts are far from Him.

Take a minute to examine your heart. How can you make sure you're worshiping God in spirit and truth rather than going through the motions?

What God taught me today and what I plan to do about it:

_____

_____

_____

_____

_____

_____

_____

GIVING GOD HIS DUE

God wants and deserves all you have.

READ 1 CHRONICLES 16:29.

First Chronicles is a book of Jewish history believed to have been written by Ezra. A Jewish leader in his day, Ezra felt a deep need to remind his people where they'd come from and how blessed they were to be God's chosen people.

Compare this verse to Psalm 29:2 (Day 19). What has been added in this verse?

What do you have to offer God? How would you describe your willingness to offer that?

What do you struggle to let go of?

Have you ever offered what is rightfully God's to someone/something else? Explain.

READ ROMANS 12:1-2.

Paul wrote these words to the Christians in Rome. He encouraged them to offer their whole selves to God in worship—not for a minute, not for a while, but for the rest of their lives. Paul called them to lay down their selfish desires, make decisions that reflect God's will instead of their own, and follow through in obedience.

Of course, the only way to do that is to find out what God's will is, and that takes time. Being limited humans, we don't think like God does, but the Holy Spirit does and will help us if we let Him. The process requires patience, focus, effort, and humility and involves a lot of trial and error, but the investment is worth it.

This passage follows a quoted hymn praising God's wisdom and knowledge. Before calling the Roman Christians to action, Paul gave them a reason to act.

What reason(s) do you have to worship God?

Are you letting the Holy Spirit transform your mind so you can figure out what God's will is, or are you just guessing at what His will might be? Explain.

Is your sacrifice "holy and pleasing" to God? How does it bring glory to Him? Explain.

What God taught me today and what I plan to do about it:

DAY 22

LOVING GOD WITH YOUR HEART AND SOUL

It's good to feel affection for God—that's the part of being a Christian everyone enjoys—but true love goes beyond affection. If your love for God is sincere, you'll serve and obey Him just like Jesus did during His ministry here on earth.

READ MARK 12:30.

This command came from Deuteronomy 6:4-5, often called the book of the law (Deut. 31:26). Those who considered themselves faithful Jews recited this multiple times throughout the day. In Mark 12:28, a scribe had asked Jesus what was the most important command. Jesus' response is recorded in verse 30.

To love God with your heart is to want more for Him than you want for yourself or anyone else. It also means you respond to Him, people, and circumstances in a way that proves your desire to see Him glorified.

Are you more worried about getting what you want and think you deserve out of life or making sure God gets what He wants and deserves out of you?

Do your thoughts, words, and actions over the past day prove the answer you just gave? Explain.

How might living for yourself while claiming to love God hinder your mission?

To love God with your soul is to dedicate your entire being—your physical self, spiritual self, emotional self, intellectual self, social self, and so on—to His glory now and for all eternity.

Have you given God control of all the areas listed above? What are some areas you still need to turn over to Him?

How will letting go of every part of yourself glorify God? What will it prove? To whom?

To Israel, Deuteronomy 6:4-5 was the foundation of God's law and covenant with them. The command in Deuteronomy began with a statement about God's character, then included instructions for responding appropriately to Him. Today, Jesus' words in Mark 12:30 still teach us and lead us in responding appropriately to Him.

How does responding appropriately to God glorify Him?

What God taught me today and what I plan to do about it:

_____

_____

_____

_____

_____

_____

_____

_____

_____

LOVING GOD WITH YOUR MIND AND STRENGTH

The heart and soul are not the only things involved in loving God—we also love Him with our minds and our strength.

READ MARK 12:30 AGAIN.

To love God with your mind is to hold God's Word up as the ultimate authority in your life, sifting through every thought that enters your consciousness and only letting thoughts that are pleasing to God and consistent with the truth of God's Word remain.

About how many minutes or hours do you devote to reading, processing, and meditating on God's Word each week? What about human wisdom?

2 hours -

Explain why focusing on human wisdom as much as you focus on God's wisdom hurts you, others, and hinders your mission.

when we focus on Human wisdom we let society sweep in and change our identity

READ ROMANS 12:2 AND EPHESIANS 4:23.

In both of these letters, Paul instructed the early church to allow the Spirit to renew their minds and transform their hearts. Although God is the only One who can change our hearts, we can choose to change our habits. The kind of renewal Paul spoke of in both of these verses requires things like prayer, reading and meditating on (or thinking deeply about) God's Word, worship, and focusing on how God works in our lives and through us by the power of the Holy Spirit.

What steps can you take to actively filter your thoughts and only let what's good and pleasing to God remain? Explain.

→ pray about EVERYTHING
⌐ ask him to take away the bad "prune your trees"

To love God with your strength is to make a physical, mental, and emotional effort to use the gifts and abilities He's given you for His glory. Loving God with our strength requires action.

We love God with all that we are. Since God gave all of Himself in His covenant with Israel and gave His Son to establish a new covenant with us, it is not unreasonable for us to respond by giving ourselves completely to Him or for Him to expect us to respond that way. All things are for His glory.

promise, deal

How are you developing all your gifts and abilities? Why do you think it's sometimes tempting to become complacent? Explain.

→ surrounding yourself w/ community
→ becoming complacent happens when we don't have deep roots.

What actions is God asking you to take? What's holding you back? What will help you as you move forward?

college/ after HS → pursuing people wholeheartedly
↳ societal views are holding me back
↳ community & looking @ who he pursued

What are you doing to make an intentional effort to use all your gifts and abilities for God's glory? What gifts and abilities are you tempted to keep to yourself? Explain.

→ serving
→ leading my girls
→ reaching out to freshies
→ being outgoing

tempted to keep for myself:
→ worship
→ sacrificial love

Why do think it's sometimes easier to leave the difficult things for someone else to do? Explain.

Because it's easy. and because when we don't have to put in as much effort it becomes easier.

What God taught me today and what I plan to do about it:

pray about everything (even the little things) and jump into every situation knowing that God's Got MY BACK!

REVIEW DAY

You've finished two chapters of daily Bible study guides. Way to go! Now it's time to look back through the Bible study guides you just completed and answer a few questions:

On a scale of 1 to 10, how much effort have you put into completing your daily Bible study guides?

How much attention have you devoted to hearing God's voice? What has He said to you?

In what ways have you tried to carry out the plans God wants you to make? How has God used your obedience?

How has living intentionally for God's glory affected you so far? How has it affected those around you?

If you are already leading a *100 Days* group, don't stop inviting people to join. Encourage group members to invite friends and family and help new group members get their own copy of *100 Days: The Glory Experiment* so they can hit the ground running.

PRAYER

- Thank God for His Word and for speaking to your heart.
- Thank Him for loving you and for the privilege of glorifying Him through obedience to His Word.
- Thank Him for any results that may have come from your obedience.
- Make any commitments you need to make going forward, and ask God for the desire and ability to follow through on those commitments.

CHAPTER THREE

JESUS THE SON

How do I glorify God through my relationship with Christ?

AS YOU GO

As you work your way through Chapter 3 of this study, you can record your questions here. Write in the answers as God gives them to you.

QUESTION	ANSWER	SCRIPTURAL PROOF

WHO JESUS IS AND WHAT HE HAS DONE

Take a minute to read through the About Jesus list on page 219 in The Truth section. As you read each statement, consider its meaning, weight, and what it has to do with you. Put a check mark by the ones that stand out to you.

Now, review the truths you checked. Write out the two truths that affect you the most and answer the questions following each one.

TRUTH 1:

What does this truth have to do with me?

How does God want me to respond to this truth? What does that look like?

How will my appropriate response glorify God and advance the gospel?

TRUTH 2:

What does this truth have to do with me?

How does God want me to respond to this truth? What does that look like?

How will my appropriate response glorify God and advance the gospel?

What God taught me today and what I plan to do about it:

BELIEVING IN JESUS

Many people claim to know and love God, but they reject Jesus. According to God's Word, you cannot love God the Father and reject Jesus the Son.

READ JOHN 3:31-36.

John the Baptist was Jesus' cousin. His sole purpose in life was to glorify God by pointing others to Jesus. When the crowd that had been following John began following Jesus instead, John's followers were upset. They wanted to promote John, not Jesus. But John assured them that Jesus deserved to be in the spotlight because He is God's Son.

According to this passage, who sent Jesus and gave Him authority? Whose words did Jesus speak?

What are some ways believing Jesus' words glorifies God?

How does God the Father feel about Jesus the Son? What did He do to prove it?

If you truly believe Jesus is who He says He is and did what He said He would do, then you know you have to make Him your boss to be saved from the consequences of sin. There's no other choice. Those who live in disobedience to God prove they don't believe in Jesus. By rejecting Him, they choose to suffer God's wrath.

Those who believe in the Son have eternal life, but that doesn't mean God won't hold them accountable for the sin they commit after giving their lives to Jesus. He is just (or fair) and can't pretend things are okay when they are not.

What are the consequences for those who reject Jesus?

John's use of the word "remains" (v. 36) implies a continual action or something to be endured. In other words, the consequences for those who reject Jesus will last a while. If those people never accept Jesus, then those consequences "remain" forever.

Does the way you respond to Jesus glorify God? Why or why not?

What God taught me today and what I plan to do about it:

REPRESENTING JESUS

Your eternal salvation is both a gift and a privilege. The moment you were saved, you became Jesus' representative here on earth. You are called to take part in His mission to seek and save the lost by sharing the gospel and living a life that illustrates the gospel's power to change sinners from the inside out.

READ 2 CORINTHIANS 5:17-21 AND 1 PETER 4:11.

Ambassadors play a very special role in public relations. Ambassadors are more than assistants; ambassadors share their sender's purpose, carry their authority, and act according to their wishes.

Describe the similarities between your role as Jesus' ambassador and the role Jesus played during His earthly ministry.

What do you have to know to fulfill your role as Jesus' ambassador? What mind-set should you have?

You operate under _____ authority and power.

What might happen if you try to do things on your own, without asking for God's help? How might this affect your mission?

READ JOHN 14:13-14.

In this passage, Jesus was talking to His disciples about what life would be like after He ascended to the Father. The disciples were understandably worried about Jesus leaving. They wanted to know where He was going, when and how they could join Him, and how they would get by until they saw Him again.

Jesus responded by reassuring His disciples that they wouldn't really be alone— He would continue to enable their ministry, and their effectiveness as His ambassadors would only increase when He ascended to heaven. Jesus promised to give His disciples whatever they asked for in His name.

This may sound like a blank check promise, one the disciples could abuse if they wanted to, but it's not. To do, say, or pray something "in Jesus' name" is to claim that our actions, attitudes, and the ultimate purpose behind them are aligned with God. Jesus was not promising to obey the disciples but to honor the requests they made in obedience to Him.

What do people tend to ask or say "in Jesus' name"? When can this be harmful?

When does acting and asking "in Jesus' name" glorify God? Explain.

What God taught me today and what I plan to do about it:

STAY FOCUSED

Jesus drew a lot of attention during His time on earth but managed to stay focused on His mission and purpose, setting an example for His ambassadors to follow.

READ JOHN 6:34-40.

Jesus spoke these words to a crowd of people who had been following Him for days. They did not necessarily follow because they believed He was the Son of God who had come to save them; they were fascinated by and benefited from His miracles. Their minds weren't on eternity, but Jesus' mind was.

Rather than basking in the attention of curious onlookers and admirers, Jesus faithfully redirected their attention to the Father. Jesus promised to save and keep forever those who were able to look beyond their temporary needs to their eternal need and put their faith in Him.

Does the way you handle attention glorify the Father? How does it affect your mission? Explain.

READ JOHN 6:44-45.

Some of those who followed Jesus during His earthly ministry had a tough time believing He came from God because they knew His family and had watched Him grow up (John 6:42). While Jesus never did or said anything that would disprove His claim to have come from God, they couldn't get past His seemingly common birth. In their eyes, Jesus was too familiar to be divine.

Rather than arguing with doubters or wasting time trying to explain the unexplainable, Jesus simply spoke the truth and left the convincing up to the Holy Spirit whose job it was to do so.

According to this passage, can you take credit on any level for your salvation? Explain.

Can you take credit for the salvation of those who put their faith in Jesus as a direct or indirect result of your obedience to God? Why or why not?

How should you respond when people compliment you or give you credit for what God accomplishes through your obedience?

What God taught me today and what I plan to do about it:

DISPLAYING JESUS' HUMILITY

If anyone had a reason to be arrogant, Jesus did. Instead, He displayed humility even in the most challenging situations. His ambassadors must do the same.

READ PHILIPPIANS 2:5-11.

This passage is considered by some to be the church's earliest hymn. In the verses that come before it, Paul instructed believers to look out for not only for their own interests, but for the interests of others (v.4). In this passage, Paul holds Jesus up as an example of how to do that.

The church in Philippi was already known for its general obedience and generosity, but Paul still presented Jesus as an example of humility.

If you wanted to describe a friend as humble, what would you say?

No matter how far we might have to lower ourselves to obey God and bring Him glory, our experience doesn't begin to compare to Jesus'. He left the perfection of heaven and the privileges that came with being one with God (John 1:1) to become a human being with next to no social standing. Out of love for us and obedience to God, Jesus became a servant and suffered a gruesome death normally reserved for criminals.

How did Jesus' humble obedience glorify God? How did God respond to it?

Humility means those of us who know Jesus should think of ourselves less often than we think of others. We should also think of Jesus more than we think of ourselves. After Jesus was humiliated on the cross, God exalted Him. The rest of the world will do the same one day, but those of us who already know Him have the privilege of doing so now.

How does approaching Jesus with humility and reverence glorify God?

READ EPHESIANS 4:2.

Humility helps believers live together in Christian community and carry out our mission in a way that glorifies God. It's not a trait possessed by some, but a responsibility given to all (Luke 14:11; Jas. 4:10).

Is having the right attitude more or less difficult than simply doing what you're told to do? Explain.

How will displaying Jesus' humility even in the most challenging situations glorify God?

What God taught me today and what I plan to do about it:

WAITING ON GLORY

Even as He carried out His mission here on earth, Jesus longed to return to the Father and enjoy the glory that was His before the world began. Still, He never assumed that glory for Himself. Instead, Jesus focused on being obedient and waited for glory to be given by the Father.

READ JOHN 8:52-55.

Jesus made many of the Jewish leaders of His day uncomfortable, so they constantly tried to discredit Him. In this passage, they accused Him of being demon-possessed.

Know this, Jesus is God (Rom. 9:5). He didn't have to stand for such accusations. Jesus could have pulled rank on the religious elite of His day, rattling off a long list of accomplishments and credentials, like God did in His conversation with Job (Job 38–41). Instead, Jesus waited patiently for His Father to reveal His identity to the right people at the right time. He was content to know and be known only by the Father if that was what the Father wanted.

Jesus showed humility before God. What did this prove? What did it accomplish?

List some ways promoting yourself might interfere with your mission to glorify God.

When will resisting the temptation to prove or defend yourself to others glorify God? Explain.

READ ROMANS 8:28-30.

Paul didn't mean God had already glorified Christians when he said "[God] also glorified." He meant it was a sure thing. Because of Jesus, Christians are able to look forward to glorification in heaven, just like Jesus did.

Whom did God conform into the image of His Son? Why?

How does it make you feel to know you'll someday share Jesus' glory in heaven?

Which means more. glory given by God or glory given by people? Why?

What are some ways this passage encourages you as you wait and work toward what's been promised?

What God taught me today and what I plan to do about it:

_____

_____

_____

_____

_____

_____

_____

LOVING JESUS

Anyone can claim to know and love Jesus, but we show our love by obeying Him and loving others.

READ JOHN 14:21,23-24.

Up until this point, Jesus' disciples followed Him faithfully and obeyed even when others turned back. However, their devotion would be tested, first when Jesus was crucified and buried and later when He ascended into heaven. Jesus spoke these words to focus and encourage the disciples against coming temptation to turn away from Him or give up on the mission—He knew obedience would be more difficult once He was no longer physically with them.

According to this passage, what shows that a person truly loves Jesus?

Sincere love for Jesus isn't something that comes and goes. It's a constant devotion and desire to know Him better that grows as we obey His commands.

What is God's response to those who love Jesus? Why do you think He responds this way?

What does our genuine love for Jesus encourage others to consider?

Highlight the second part of verse 24. How does our continual love for Jesus glorify God and advance the gospel?

READ JOHN 14:23; 16:27.

The word for love in John 14:23 is *agape*, which is intentional, compassionate love expressed through service and/or meeting a need. This love is based on the giver's character and intentions, not the recipient's worth. God showed *agape* to all sinners through Jesus' sacrifice on the cross (John 3:16).

The word for love in John 16:27 is *phileo*, which refers to the love we have for our friends; this is more sentimental. According to these verses, God makes friends with those who love His Son through service and obedience.

What common goal or interest does God share with those who truly love Jesus?

Does it make sense that God befriends those who love Jesus? Why or why not?

How does displaying confidence in God's friendship glorify Him and advance the gospel?

What God taught me today and what I plan to do about it:

_____

_____

_____

_____

_____

_____

_____

REMAINING IN JESUS' LOVE

Obeying Jesus doesn't get easier, but the more we get to know Him, the more our desire to obey Him increases.

READ JOHN 15:9-12.

Jesus seems to imply that if we disobey Him, He will stop loving us, but that's not actually what He said. Disobedience causes relational static between you and God, making it difficult for you to communicate with Him or bear spiritual fruit (Prov. 28:9; John 15:4)—but it won't make Jesus stop loving you. Remember, God's love for humankind is *agape* love. It can't be earned, so it can't be lost.

Jesus' words here are a promise of blessing, not a threat. Remaining in Jesus' love means having the same attitude toward God and others that Jesus had during His earthly ministry. When we follow Jesus as our model, we enjoy a deeper level of fellowship with God than those who follow with less enthusiasm.

The key to remaining in Jesus' love is obedience. When you obey God, He works and reveals Himself through your obedience. The more you obey Him, the more you learn about Him. The more you learn about Him, the better you're able to represent Him. The better you represent Him, the deeper your friendship with Him grows.

What command did Jesus give in this passage?

Is this command always easy for you to follow? Why or why not?

When is it tempting for you to stop obeying this command? Explain.

What can you do when loving others (agape) becomes difficult?

How will choosing to remain in Jesus' love glorify God and advance the gospel?

What God taught me today and what I plan to do about it:

BEING JESUS' FRIEND

Friendship with Jesus is costly, but no price is too high to pay for the privilege.

READ JOHN 15:12-14.

The disciples were more than simple acquaintances of Jesus and had already proven themselves to be more committed than any of the other people who'd followed Him to this point. They probably already considered themselves to be His friends. Jesus wanted to prepare them for His physical absence.

Describe how Jesus displayed His love for God and mankind.

List some ways we can demonstrate our love for Jesus in return. What does loving others have to do with showing our love for Jesus?

Are you willing to love others as Jesus loved you? Is friendship with Jesus worth the cost? Why or why not?

How does your friendship with Jesus glorify God?

READ JOHN 21:15-22.

After Jesus' resurrection, He appeared to Peter three times before He ascended to heaven. Peter denied knowing Jesus—his best friend and the One he had promised to follow no matter what—when He was arrested. Even so, Jesus extended mercy and grace to Peter, putting his heart and mind at ease. By the time this conversation occurred, no doubt Peter was eager to do anything Jesus asked of him to prove his devotion.

What did Jesus ask of Peter?

What would Peter's obedience prove? What would it accomplish in the long run?

Why wouldn't Jesus tell Peter what the future held for John? What did He want Peter to focus on?

Resisting the temptation to compare God's plan for your life to His plan for others' lives glorifies Him. What three steps can you take this week to pursue God's specific plan for your life?

What God taught me today and what I plan to do about it:

DAY 34

REVIEW DAY

Congratulations! You've completed one-third of the daily Bible study guides. Before you move on, take a minute to look back through the guides in this chapter and answer the following questions:

On a scale of 1 to 10, how much effort have you put into completing your daily Bible study guides?

How much attention have you devoted to hearing God's voice? What has He said to you?

How has living intentionally for God's glory affected you so far? How has it affected those around you?

If you're already leading a *100 Days* group, don't be surprised if individuals in your group leave to start their own groups with brand new members. Instead, be glad they've chosen to step up and reach out to the people around them for God's glory. Fight the urge to compete and compare in the days ahead. Encourage them. Pray for them. Fill the gaps they leave behind by inviting new people to join you and encourage the rest of your group members to do the same.

PRAYER

- Thank God for His Word and for speaking to your heart.
- Thank Him for loving you and for the privilege of glorifying Him through your obedience to His Word.
- Thank Him for any results that may have come from your obedience.
- Make any commitments you need to make going forward and ask God for the desire and ability to follow through on those commitments.

CHAPTER FOUR

THE HOLY SPIRIT

How do I glorify God in my relationship with the Holy Spirit?

AS YOU GO

As you work your way through Chapter 4 of this study, you can record your questions here. Write in the answers when God gives them to you.

QUESTION	ANSWER	SCRIPTURAL PROOF

WHO THE HOLY SPIRIT IS AND WHAT HE DOES

Check out the About the Holy Spirit list on page 220 included in The Truth section of this book. As you read each statement, consider its meaning, weight, and what it has to do with you. Put a check mark next to the ones that stand out to you.

Now, review the truths you checked. Write out the two truths that affect you the most and answer the questions following each one.

TRUTH 1:

What does this truth have to do with me?

How does God want me to respond to this truth? What does that look like?

How will my appropriate response glorify God and advance the gospel?

TRUTH 2:

What does this truth have to do with me?

How does God want me to respond to this truth? What does that look like?

How will my appropriate response glorify God and advance the gospel?

What God taught me today and what I plan to do about it:

_____

_____

_____

_____

_____

_____

_____

_____

_____

_____

_____

_____

_____

_____

_____

_____

_____

PARTNERING WITH JESUS

All members of the Trinity—God the Father, Jesus the Son, and the Holy Spirit—work together toward the same goal. They work toward God's glory.

READ JOHN 14:8-14.

Once the events leading to Jesus' arrest and crucifixion were set in motion, Jesus began to speak to His disciples with a sense of urgency. He explained the abstract truth of His relationship to and with the Father, His disciples' relationship to and with God, and the role of the Holy Spirit in all of it—all to prepare His disciples for life on earth without His physical presence.

What did Jesus reveal about His relationship to and with the Father?

Jesus acted under _____ power and authority. What proof did He offer?

What expectation did Jesus express about the works of those who believe in Him (v. 12)?

What power and authority would they be acting under? What ultimate purpose did Jesus point to (v. 13)?

What would their obedience prove to those around them? How would this glorify God?

If you're a Christian, your relationship to God the Father, Jesus the Son, and the Holy Spirit is the same relationship Jesus' disciples had. So, Jesus' words to them in this passage are also His words to you.

There was only one Jesus while He walked the earth, but there are now many who operate under His authority and by His power through the Holy Spirit.

What key factor set the stage for "greater works" to be done once Jesus ascended? Explain.

How does your obedience to the Holy Spirit glorify the Father?

What God taught me today and what I plan to do about it:

COMFORT IN THE HOLY SPIRIT

If you're a Christian, you don't ever need to feel alone. The Holy Spirit lives inside you, making it possible for you to enjoy miraculous and constant intimacy with God no matter what's happening in your life.

READ JOHN 14:15-20.

The disciples knew they were about to be separated from Jesus, but they weren't sure how, when, or for how long. They were probably nervous. However, Jesus knew how things would play out and comforted them by explaining what He could.

What emotion do you detect in Jesus' words? What does this tell you about His attitude toward the disciples?

What does this tell you about His attitude toward you as His disciple?

When Jesus ascended and the Counselor came, He set Christians apart from everyone else. They thought and acted like no one else because they had what no one else had: God's power within them and the ability to communicate directly with Him. These things definitely gave them an advantage over others in many ways, but might also have made them seem odd to people who didn't know Jesus.

Would you rather be a misunderstood disciple with the Counselor living inside of you or someone who misunderstands because you don't have the Counselor? Explain.

How is having the Counselor with you all the time better than walking next to Jesus as the disciples did?

List some practical ways knowing the Holy Spirit is always with you affects the way you think and feel.

How should it affect the way you face challenges and uncertainty?

How will agreeing with and obeying the Holy Spirit glorify God and advance the gospel?

What God taught me today and what I plan to do about it:

BEARING SPIRITUAL FRUIT

Many people who claim to be Christians aren't. Christians are recognizable because they obey the Holy Spirit and bear spiritual fruit.

READ JOHN 15:5-8,16.

Remaining in Jesus means obeying Him completely, depending on the Holy Spirit to guide and empower you through that obedience. Only those who put their faith in Jesus have the Holy Spirit, so only those who belong to Him can remain in Him.

List some indicators that a person truly belongs to Jesus Christ. List some indicators that a person does not belong to Jesus.

According to these verses, what keeps a Christian from being successful in advancing the gospel?

Why is the idea of being useless for advancing the gospel so scary to those who truly love God? How can we avoid this?

What promise did Jesus make to those who choose to remain in Him?

Apart from Jesus, we can do nothing, that includes bearing spiritual fruit. But we shouldn't be discouraged by that. God empowers those who walk according to His will and seek His glory. If you make the effort to produce spiritual fruit like He wants you to, you can be certain He will make sure it happens by the power of His Spirit.

READ GALATIANS 5:19-25.

In this passage, Paul pointed out the difference between those who live for and by themselves and those who live for and by the power of God. Paul provided these instructions so the Galatian Christians would know whom to listen to and how to behave with the help of the Holy Spirit.

According to these verses, what enables a person to show these character traits all at once and with consistency?

What does remaining in Jesus have to do with a person exhibiting these traits?

Ask the Holy Spirit to guide you as you examine your heart. Are you bearing spiritual fruit? Why or why not?

Which of these traits is most difficult for you? Which one is easiest? Explain.

How might a lack of spiritual fruit in your life interfere with your mission to glorify God?

What God taught me today and what I plan to do about it:

_____

_____

_____

_____

RECEIVING CORRECTION

It's a privilege (not a shame or embarrassment) to experience the conviction, or convincing, of the Holy Spirit.

Before you become a Christian, the Holy Spirit's conviction is proof that God desires a relationship with you. After you become a Christian, the activity of the Holy Spirit in your life proves that you're a child of God forever. It proves that God loves you, cares about your spiritual growth, and wants to use you in His mission to rescue the lost.

READ EPHESIANS 1:3-6.

The first two chapters of Paul's letter to the church in Ephesus encourage Christians to remember where we came from, what God has done for us through Jesus Christ, and where we're headed as His permanently adopted children. These passages are rich with gospel truth and inspire to action those who've been saved through faith by God's grace.

If you're a Christian, how does it affect you to know that God chose you for adoption before the world was ever created?

What is your response to knowing it pleased God to adopt you?

READ JOHN 6:44.

When did you first experience the Holy Spirit directing you toward God?

Describe what your life would be like now if that had never happened.

READ JOHN 16:7-8.

This passage is part of Jesus' commentary on the abstract concept of the very real Holy Spirit who would indwell the disciples in His physical absence. This is the same Holy Spirit who indwells those who put their faith in Jesus Christ for salvation today.

What role of the Holy Spirit is described in these verses?

What does the Holy Spirit, as Counselor, do (v. 8)?

If the Holy Spirit hadn't helped you understand sin and its consequences and then convicted you of your own sin, it would have been impossible for you to surrender your life to Jesus.

How might resisting the Holy Spirit's correction prevent your spiritual growth or ability to bear spiritual fruit? How would that affect your mission?

How does allowing the Holy Spirit to convict you of your sin glorify God?

What God taught me today and what I plan to do about it:

RESPONDING TO CORRECTION

Conviction by the Holy Spirit is beneficial, but guilt stirred by the enemy is destructive.

READ 2 CORINTHIANS 7:10.

This verse occurs in the middle of a passage where Paul expressed relief over the Corinthian Christians' appropriate response to the Holy Spirit's correction. To make sure they continued to do so, he pointed out all the good that came from it.

Conviction and guilt are two very different things. Conviction is of the Holy Spirit, but guilt is of Satan—the enemy of God and His children. Conviction is offered in love, but guilt is dealt with evil intent. Conviction leads to freedom from the sin that weighs people down and keeps them from experiencing all God wants for them, but guilt leads to fear and spiritual paralysis. Although conviction and guilt both cause sorrow, the sorrow of conviction is temporary and ends in joy while the sorrow caused by guilt continues and controls.

What should you do when the Holy Spirit shows you something in your life that doesn't glorify God? Why?

What might cause a person to resist the Holy Spirit's conviction?

What would their resistance say about what they believe or what they value most?

How can you tell the difference between conviction and guilt? List some ways you can respond to each one.

READ 1 JOHN 1:9.

The same John who wrote the gospel by that name wrote 1, 2, and 3 John. He wrote 1 John to encourage Christians all over the world to stand up for and cling to the gospel, exercise spiritual discernment, and guard their hearts against persecution and false teaching. This affectionate letter communicates John's sincere concern for the spiritual and emotional well-being of his younger brothers and sisters in the faith.

What does God promise to do when we respond appropriately to the conviction of the Holy Spirit?

What freedom and/or relief does this promise bring you?

How does confessing our sin glorify God?

What God taught me today and what I plan to do about it:

DEMONSTRATING CONFIDENCE IN THE HOLY SPIRIT

If our eternal salvation and future in heaven depended on us, we'd have reason to worry; thankfully, it doesn't. Those of us who've put our faith in Jesus Christ for salvation can have confidence in our future with Him.

READ 2 CORINTHIANS 1:20-22.

Whose power enables a Christ-follower to live a life that pleases God?

Highlight the phrase "every one of God's promises is 'Yes' in him" (v. 20). What does this tell you about the confidence believers should have about their salvation and eternity with Christ?

What assurance do you have that you're saved and will spend eternity in heaven (v. 22)?

Do you have any reason to doubt that your eternity is secure, according to these verses? Explain.

What God did through Jesus Christ was His greatest masterpiece, tying the past covenants to future glory and our hearts to His forever. An extravagant gesture, it showed everyone once and for all who He is, what He's capable of, and why He should be lifted up in our lives. If we are ever tempted to doubt God, all we need to do is think about the gospel and remember what we know to be true: He never fails. In Him, we find the answer and solution to every problem and the confidence to say "Amen."

How does living in confidence of God's ability to save and keep you forever glorify Him?

READ HEBREWS 5:13–6:3.

The author of Hebrews expressed the idea that these believers should be more mature in their faith. The letter suggests that these believers were turning to Jewish rituals that were no longer necessary because of Christ. So, the author encouraged them to remember the truth of who Christ is and what He has done for us.

What topics were these believers focused on, according to this passage?

What are some problems their misplaced focus likely caused in sharing the gospel? When do you face similar temptations in your own life?

How might spiritual immaturity hinder your mission? How will your spiritual growth glorify God?

What God taught me today and what I plan to do about it:

_____

_____

_____

_____

_____

_____

_____

WITH THE HOLY SPIRIT

Spiritual growth is a joint effort between Christians and the Holy Spirit. If you're waiting on the Holy Spirit to do it all for you, you're going nowhere.

READ 2 PETER 1:3-11.

Peter wrote to encourage new Christians all over the world to be bold and obedient as they learned how to live out their faith in Jesus Christ. He knew what they were capable of by the power of the Holy Spirit even if they didn't quite understand how it all worked yet. Inspired by the work God had done in his own life, Peter reminded new Christians of all they had in Christ and what was possible if they chose to apply what they'd been given.

What encouraging truth do you find in verse three?

Why might new Christians find this truth particularly encouraging?

What two reasons did Peter give for God sending the Holy Spirit to live inside of believers (v. 4)?

Before people become Christians, most of the truth they receive comes from outside sources at a pace determined by others. They don't yet know what they need, so they don't go looking for it. When people become Christians, they should seek the truth for themselves so God can use it to grow them. They still may not know exactly what they need, but God does, and He teaches those who are willing and eager to learn (1 John 2:27).

Take a minute to examine your heart. If you are a Christian, are you taking full advantage of the Holy Spirit's presence in your life? Explain.

What role do we play in our own spiritual growth? Where should we focus our attention and efforts? Why?

What happens to Christians who don't focus their attention and efforts on these things?

Notice all the ways Peter mentioned to "supplement your faith" (vv. 5-8). Which of these are most difficult for you? Why?

How will growing your faith and living out these qualities glorify God? (Hint: Check out verse 8.)

What God taught me today and what I plan to do about it:

_____

_____

_____

_____

_____

_____

_____

LEARNING FROM THE HOLY SPIRIT

The Holy Spirit never contradicts what Jesus taught during His earthly ministry or any other truth found in God's Word. Instead, the Holy Spirit helps us understand Jesus' teachings and God's Word in a way we never could on our own.

READ JOHN 14:26.

During His earthly ministry, Jesus made a special effort to point things out to His twelve apostles, explain His parables, and tell them what was to come. In the moment, they didn't understand it all, but once Jesus had ascended back into heaven, they did. The Holy Spirit revealed it to them when they were ready, helped them process it, and used it to guide their future actions.

What two specific things does the Holy Spirit do, according to this verse?

How does it encourage you that part of the Holy Spirit's job is to help you know God better and understand how to live for Him?

What is something about God you need the Spirit's help to understand?

READ JOHN 16:13.

Some Christians think it would be easier to hear from and obey Jesus if they could walk with Him in the flesh like His disciples did, but that's not necessarily true.

Jesus reassured the disciples that the relationship they would have with Him after His ascension would be even better than the one they had with Him during His earthly ministry—He would speak directly to their hearts through the Holy Spirit.

Why was it so important for the disciples to understand that the Holy Spirit would speak only what was from God?

How might this information have protected them from people who didn't know Jesus, but claimed to hear from the Holy Spirit as well?

READ JOHN 10:27.

Jesus' voice is unlike any other. Those who belong to God are able to pick it out from all the other voices that fight for their attention. Of course, this skill takes practice. The more time we spend listening to His voice by reading God's Word and praying, the easier it will be to shut out the noise and focus on the One who leads us to a life of safety and productivity for God's glory.

In what ways has relying on the Holy Spirit helped you understand God's truth and advance the gospel?

What might happen if you don't practice listening for Jesus' voice?

How might relying on feelings and hunches keep you from glorifying God?

What God taught me today and what I plan to do about it:

_____

_____

_____

_____

RELYING ON THE HOLY SPIRIT FOR DISCERNMENT

Resist the influence of those who don't know Jesus. Because they're not driven by the Holy Spirit they can't comprehend the things of God, much less help you discern God's will for your life.

READ 1 CORINTHIANS 2:6-16.

Surrounded by commercialism, greed, and immorality, the Corinthian Christians struggled to maintain their spiritual focus and resist temptation, sometimes allowing the sinful practices of their culture to creep into their lives. In this passage, the apostle Paul stressed the importance of ignoring the arguments and advice of those who don't follow Christ.

Judging by Paul's arguments in this passage, what do you think the Corinthian Christians had been hearing from their peers and community leaders?

What kind of conflict might this have created in their hearts and minds?

Which is better, according to this passage: human wisdom or God's wisdom? Why?

With whom does God share His wisdom? How?

What reassurance(s) did Paul offer those determined to obey God in spite of what anyone else might say?

What are some ways you relate to the Corinthian Christians?

How might remembering that the Holy Spirit lives inside you help you resist temptation and stay spiritually focused?

How can remembering what the Holy Spirit is accomplishing in you help you stay spiritually focused?

Describe how maintaining your spiritual focus and ignoring the spiritual input and advice of those who don't know Jesus glorifies God.

What God taught me today and what I plan to do about it:

_____

_____

_____

_____

_____

_____

_____

_____

_____

_____

_____

DEPENDING ON THE HOLY SPIRIT FOR DIRECTION

God has a plan for your life. If you stay tuned in to the Holy Spirit, He will reveal it to you and give you the strength you need to obey.

READ ISAIAH 30:21.

In this verse, the prophet Isaiah encouraged God's people to depend on God for direction and guidance. God is faithful to guide His people through His Word and through His Spirit. He doesn't leave us without direction, but gives us what we need to stay on the right path.

One of the Holy Spirit's functions is reminding Christians of Jesus' words. What's one way you can increase the likelihood that you'll hear the Holy Spirit when He speaks?

The Holy Spirit never contradicts the truth of God's Word. What can you do to test whether the voice you hear, the tug you feel, or the hunch you have is actually from God?

What should you do when the choice you want to make doesn't line up with God's Word and God's will for your life?

List some steps you can take when you aren't sure if your choice is God's will for your life.

How will submitting to God in the decisions you make bring Him glory?

READ EPHESIANS 2:10.

Before people ever become Christians, they glorify God by bearing His image on the outside. When people become Christians, God takes that framework and transforms it from the inside out, fashioning it to fulfill a certain purpose within the kingdom to which it now belongs. To ignore God's specific plan for your life is to fail to live up to your potential in the kingdom.

What blessing(s) might you miss if you tune Him out or become distracted by your own methods and desires?

READ ISAIAH 40:29-31.

Everyone gets tired, and everyone gets discouraged. To pretend you don't is to rob God of the opportunity to glorify Himself through the frailty of your human form. The miraculous happens not when you pretend to be unaffected by the pressures of life, but when you allow God to work in, through, and in spite of those pressures and empower you to do what people in similar situations without God cannot.

Does this passage promise Christians an easier life than others have? Explain.

What does this passage actually promise?

How will relying on God's strength when you are weary glorify Him?

What God taught me today and what I plan to do about it:

DAY 46

APPRECIATING THE GIFTS OF THE SPIRIT

A unified team working together effectively and self-sacrificially toward the common goal of winning is evidence of good coaching. Similarly, a unified group of Christians working together effectively and self-sacrificially for God's glory is evidence of God's power to transform and faithfulness to sustain.

READ 1 CORINTHIANS 12:4-11.

In this passage, Paul encouraged the Corinthian Christians to cooperate with one another, coordinating and using their spiritual gifts for God's glory. We don't get to pick our spiritual gifts, and that's what makes our productivity so miraculous. Without any forethought or effort on our own part, we fit together perfectly as a group. When we cooperate, each person doing what he or she was uniquely designed to do, God's purposes are accomplished no matter what. No other group can claim that.

List some of the gifts Paul mentioned.

Where do spiritual gifts come from according to this passage? For what purpose? By whose power?

The same Holy Spirit indwells every Christ-follower. Can any spiritual gift be more important than another? Why or why not?

Being unified in the Spirit doesn't mean we're all the same. What are some benefits to different believers being gifted differently?

You can't develop gifts you don't know you have, which is why Christians should make every effort to find out what gifts they've been given. Taking a spiritual gifts survey is helpful, but there's no substitute for experience. Those who volunteer readily and widely are often the first to discover their abilities and how/where God wants to use them.

When have you been tempted to wish for another believer's gift rather than obediently using the gifts God has given to you?

Remember that God's wisdom is greater than ours. In what ways can it be harmful to question God's wisdom and decision in distributing those gifts?

How will expressing equal appreciation for the spiritual gifts of those around you glorify God?

What God taught me today and what I plan to do about it:

_____

_____

_____

_____

_____

_____

_____

_____

_____

_____

DEVELOPING AND USING YOUR SPIRITUAL GIFTS

God blesses you with spiritual gifts so you can bless others in His name. They're for sharing, not hoarding.

READ HEBREWS 2:2-4.

What is the purpose of spiritual gifts according to this passage?

How does the existence of supernatural spiritual gifts in ordinary, imperfect people glorify God?

READ 2 TIMOTHY 1:6-7.

Second Timothy is a farewell letter written by the apostle Paul to his son in the faith, a young church leader named Timothy. Suspecting that he would soon be martyred—killed for his faith in Jesus Christ—Paul asked Timothy to stay strong and focused in the days ahead. Specifically, Paul told him to watch out for false teaching and to develop and use the spiritual gifts he'd been given to lead, guide, and raise up others who will stand firm in the gospel.

Who is responsible for developing the spiritual gift(s) that the Holy Spirit distributes?

Paul instructed Timothy to "rekindle" the gift God had given to him. This doesn't mean Timothy's spiritual fire was burning out; instead, Paul wanted Timothy to continue to build the spiritual fire within to do the work God had called him to do.

What do power, love, and sound judgment have to do with developing spiritual gifts?

Who provides these essential resources?

What are some ways neglecting to develop and/or use your spiritual gifts might hinder your mission and/or affect those around you? Explain.

How will developing your spiritual gifts glorify God?

What God taught me today and what I plan to do about it:

_____

_____

_____

_____

_____

_____

_____

_____

_____

_____

EMBRACING JOY

Christianity is not a feel-good faith by any stretch of the imagination. In fact, much of what Christians experience when they live boldly for Christ doesn't feel good at all, but we persevere because we know the gospel is true. The Holy Spirit's presence in our hearts proves that truth and helps us to stand strong.

READ ROMANS 15:13.

What blessings did Paul say God gives to those who trust in Him? By what power?

If you choose not to embrace these blessings in a way that others can see, do you think that will negatively affect your mission? Why or why not?

How might verbally giving God credit for the presence of these blessings in your life glorify Him?

READ JOHN 16:20-24.

> HAPPINESS: A FLEETING EMOTION BASED ON CHANGING CIRCUMSTANCES

Throughout the New Testament, the word *joy* is used to express satisfaction in response to the truth of the gospel and its power to redeem and transform. Because the gospel is lasting and true, the joy that Christians feel is also lasting and true. This sets our joy apart and above happiness. Christians' joy is made complete when they see evidence that the gospel which changed them has come full circle and transformed the life of another person, as a direct or indirect result of their obedience.

Jesus spoke these words to His disciples in anticipation of His death and eventual ascension into Heaven.

What kind of pain did Jesus have to endure for your salvation? (Review John 18–19 if you need a reminder.)

What joy came from Jesus' pain? For whom?

Have you experienced any personal pain as a result of putting your faith in Jesus Christ for salvation? Explain.

Examine your heart. Do you believe your salvation is worth the cost you've paid? Why or why not?

Can you experience the kind of joy Jesus talks about if you don't take an active role in His mission to seek and save the lost? Why or why not?

In what ways might an absence of observable joy in your life affect your mission to glorify God?

How will taking an active role in Jesus' mission and expressing the joy that you experience as a result glorify God?

What God taught me today and what I plan to do about it:

EMBRACING PEACE AND HOPE

The Holy Spirit enables Christians to respond to people and circumstances differently than they would be able to without the Holy Spirit.

READ JOHN 14:25-27.

Jesus spent a lot of time preparing His disciples for His return to the Father (Jesus' ascension). He comforted and encouraged them even before He left with the news of the Spirit who would come when He returned to the Father. If you are a Christian, His words to them are His words to you.

What does the Holy Spirit's presence in your life guarantee?

What effect does this guarantee have on your frame of mind, the way you interact with people, and the way you respond to situations right now?

Describe some ways the peace Jesus gives is different from the peace the world gives.

How might allowing present circumstances to steal the peace you've found in Jesus Christ affect your mission?

What will having a peaceful spirit even when pushed or challenged prove and to whom? How will that glorify God?

READ ROMANS 5:1-5.

The hope Christians experience is unwavering confidence in the promise of eternal salvation through Jesus Christ. Our hope is founded on evidence of the Holy Spirit's presence in our lives.

How does the hope you have in Jesus Christ strengthen you against the arguments of those who oppose the gospel?

List some ways your hope in Christ helps you to face difficulties and persecution.

What are some ways worrying about death and eternity, either privately or publicly, might compromise your mission to glorify God? Explain.

How does expressing hope in all circumstances and enthusiasm for heaven glorify God? How does this advance the gospel?

What God taught me today and what I plan to do about it:

_____

_____

_____

_____

_____

_____

_____

PRAYING IN THE SPIRIT

Prayer, or conversation with God, can be a powerful tool when practiced faithfully by Christians who understand the unique connection they have to the Father through the Holy Spirit.

READ 1 THESSALONIANS 5:17.

Paul and Timothy had to leave Thessalonica earlier than they wanted to. Concerned about the health of the brand new church they'd left behind, Paul sent Timothy back to see how the Christians there were doing. Timothy's good report prompted Paul to write 1 Thessalonians, a letter of praise and encouragement.

When and how often should Christians pray?

Paul wasn't telling the Corinthians to pray 24 hours a day, but to consistently build a strong prayer life that would support a strong faith.

READ EPHESIANS 6:18-20.

If every Christian prayed for every prayer request they ever received until the issue was resolved, nothing else would ever get done. The only way to make sure you are spending your prayer time the way God wants you to is to stay alert and attentive to His voice. If He calls your attention to something, pray about it and move on until He calls your attention to it again or brings up something else. The important thing is to pray.

What did Paul say Christians could and should pray for and about?

What most often keeps or discourages you from praying? Why?

READ ROMANS 8:26-27.

Some people are afraid to pray in front of others until they've had plenty of practice, but there's no reason anyone should hesitate to pray in front of God. He's neither surprised nor frustrated by inexperience or lack of skill.

Does a Christian have to know what or how to pray to be heard and understood by God? Explain.

Who helps us communicate with God, the One "who searches our hearts" (v. 27)? What makes Him such an effective go-between?

Keeping these things in mind, consider Ephesians 6:18-20 again. What do you suppose it means to pray in the Spirit?

How will your willingness to pray openly about anything and everything all the time glorify God and accomplish your mission?

What God taught me today and what I plan to do about it:

_____

_____

_____

_____

_____

_____

GETTING A "YES" FROM GOD

God enjoys blessing you (Deut. 30:9), but He doesn't exist to serve you. The point of prayer is not to bend God to your will, but to understand Him better with the help of the Holy Spirit so you can bend your will to His.

Don't expect God to give you everything you ask for. Though there is no formula for prayer, there are ways to tell when you aren't asking for the right things or aren't asking in the right way.

READ JAMES 4:2-3.

The Book of James—written by James, Jesus' half-brother—serves as a how-to manual for anyone who wants to live a life that glorifies God.

What are two possible reasons Christians may not receive the "yes" from God they hope for?

What ultimate purpose do all Christians share? What are impure motives?

How can you tell whether or not the motives behind your prayers are pure?

READ 1 JOHN 3:21-22.

These verses do not mean our prayers act as a magic wish list to God. No, we don't get everything we ask for; however, when we boldly ask for things that align with God's will and purpose, He is faithful to give us what we need to carry out what He has called us to do.

What kind of behavior does God expect from His children?

Why would it be good for you if God withheld what you asked for because it wasn't aligned with His will? When have you experienced this?

In what ways would God giving rebellious children everything they ask for undermine His purposes and affect the spread of the gospel message?

The Holy Spirit helps us pray in accordance with God's will. How does this encourage you?

What God taught me today and what I plan to do about it:

GROWING THROUGH PRAYER

Like any other spiritual discipline or practice, prayer brings about spiritual growth in those who regularly pray with God's glory in mind.

READ 1 JOHN 5:14-15.

What kind of prayers did John say God always hears and answers with a "yes"?

If God is already working all things together for the purpose of His will, which is His own glory (Eph. 1:11), why do you think He commands us to pray?

How can you make sure your prayers are in line with God's will?

What can you learn from the yeses you receive? What can you learn from the noes?

What do you have to want more than anything else to consistently submit to God's will in prayer?

READ JOHN 14:12-14.

Remember that to do, say, or pray something "in Jesus' name" is to say we believe our actions, attitudes, and the ultimate purpose behind them to be aligned with God.

Just to review, what is Jesus' ultimate purpose? How is God's ultimate purpose served when Jesus honors prayers in His name?

What are some ways you can be sure Jesus approves not only of what you're asking for, but also the way you're asking for it?

How should you respond when God says "no" to your prayers? When He says "yes"?

How will being obedient either way improve your prayer life?

Why might a failure to reflect on your prayers and God's answers to them slow your personal spiritual growth and/or influence your mission?

How will your conscious effort to pray according to His will glorify God?

What God taught me today and what I plan to do about it:

_____

_____

_____

_____

_____

DAY 53

FLEEING TEMPTATION

Sin might be fun for a while, but its effects are devastating both for those who haven't put their faith in Jesus yet and for those who have.

Other than setting in motion events that could bring negative consequences, sin makes it difficult for Christians to communicate with God and causes grief to the Holy Spirit inside them. This is enough reason for those who truly love God to avoid sin at all costs, even if they think they could stand the natural consequences of their own actions.

READ PSALM 66:18-19 AND PROVERBS 28:9.

Why must God ignore the prayers of Christians who are aware of their sin but refuse to turn away from sin and turn toward God?

What are some ways continuing to sin even after the Holy Spirit has convicted you might negatively impact your mission?

How will turning away from sin to keep the lines of communication with God open glorify Him? Why or why not?

READ EPHESIANS 4:30.

To "grieve" the Holy Spirit is to cause Him discomfort and limit or quiet His influence in your life.

Taking into consideration the grace God showed in sending the Holy Spirit to live inside His children to begin with, what makes a Christian's choice to continue in sin after being convicted so offensive?

Which bothers you more, the idea of hurting the Holy Spirit or the possibility that He might not minister in and through you as He has in the past?

READ 1 CORINTHIANS 10:13.

What kinds of excuses do you make for giving in to temptation?

Do your excuses make sense in light of this verse? Why or why not?

The Holy Spirit helps you discern God's will for your life. What can you do to make sure you recognize the escape routes God provides?

How will resisting temptation glorify God and advance the gospel?

What God taught me today and what I plan to do about it:

_____

_____

_____

_____

_____

_____

_____

_____

DAY 54

REVIEW DAY

You're over halfway through the *100 Days* experiment!

Before you move on, spend a little time looking back through the Bible study guides for this section (the longest one so far) and answer the following questions:

On a scale of 1 to 10, how much effort have you put into completing your daily Bible study guides?

How much attention have you devoted to hearing God's voice? What has He said to you?

How has living intentionally for God's glory affected you so far? How has it affected those around you?

If you are leading a *100 Days* group that has gotten so big it needs to split to allow for deeper discussion or to give everyone a chance to talk, choose a person (people) to lead a break-off group(s) and allow group members to choose which group they will join. Doing so will ensure that splitting doesn't slow any momentum you've gained. Splitting groups must be handled with care. Please see The Discipleship Group Guide for detailed instructions.

PRAYER

- Thank God for His Word and for speaking to your heart.
- Thank Him for loving you and for the privilege of glorifying Him through your obedience to His Word.
- Thank Him for any results that may have come from your obedience.
- Make any commitments you need to make going forward, and ask God for the desire and ability to follow through on those commitments.

CHAPTER FIVE

THE BIBLE

How do I glorify God in the way I treat His Word?

AS YOU GO

As you work your way through Chapter 5 of this study, you can record your
questions here. Write in the answers when God gives them to you.

QUESTION	ANSWER	SCRIPTURAL PROOF

DAY 55

THE INSPIRED WORD OF GOD

The Bible is more than a book; it's the inspired Word of God recorded by men. The Bible is a lifeline to those who belong to Him, revealing His character, communicating His will, and facilitating intimate communication with Him by the power of the Holy Spirit. The Holy Spirit also helps us understand God's Word and remember what it says.

READ 2 TIMOTHY 3:16-17.

Scripture is another term for the content of God's Word, the Bible.

Who wrote the Bible according to this passage? How much of it?

Who is the Bible's intended audience? How are we supposed to use it?

What happens when we use the Bible correctly?

What ultimate purpose might this outcome serve? How?

Do you revere the Bible as your ultimate authority, or do you consider it just one of many equally valuable resources? Explain.

Does your response to and use of the Bible glorify God? Why or why not?

Based on your answer, what kinds of changes might you need to make?

READ 2 PETER 1:20-21.

What part did man play in recording Scripture (v. 21)?

Why is it so important for people to understand that the Bible came from God, not from man?

How will helping them understand this glorify God?

What God taught me today and what I plan to do about it:

_____

_____

_____

_____

_____

_____

_____

_____

_____

_____

THE BIBLE DESCRIBED

Just as God is perfect, His Word is perfect.

The Bible was recorded over time by many different men with unique experiential backgrounds, personalities, and writing styles. However, just as the gospel itself doesn't change when we tell it, the absolute truth of God's Word didn't change when they wrote it down. The Bible can and should be trusted.

READ ISAIAH 40:8.

What does this verse say about God's Word? Can this be said of anything else you devote time and effort to? Explain.

How does devoting time and effort to God's Word glorify Him?

When you devote your time and effort to God's Word, what does that show others?

READ PSALM 119:160.

What does the first line of this verse say about the Bible?

Do you believe it? Why or why not?

Where do you go first when you have questions, need guidance, or need to verify the truth of something? What does this say about your trust in the Bible?

How does seeking counsel and the absolute truth from the Bible glorify God?

READ ISAIAH 55:10-11.

What word would you use to describe God's Word using only this passage as a reference?

How does God's Word glorify Him according to this passage?

Knowing that God's Word never fails to glorify Him, to what degree should you depend on it?

What God taught me and what I plan to do about it:

_____

_____

_____

_____

_____

_____

_____

_____

_____

_____

THE BIBLE'S ROLE IN THE GOSPEL

The Bible acts as an alarm that alerts people to the presence and danger of sin.

READ ROMANS 5:12-14.

> THE LAW GIVEN THROUGH MOSES REFERS TO THE TEN COMMANDMENTS; HOWEVER, MANY LAWS WERE ALSO GIVEN IN THE BOOK OF DEUTERONOMY AND THROUGHOUT THE OLD TESTAMENT. THESE WERE SUPPOSED TO REGULATE THE LIVES OF THOSE WHO HAVE A RELATIONSHIP WITH GOD.

Until God revealed His will for mankind through Moses in the form of the law, sin just was. People practiced it without fully understanding what they were doing, when they were doing it, or the negative effect it had on them. To a certain degree, they were ignorant (but not innocent).

The law put an end to all that. For the first time since Adam, the last man who had broken an actual God-given rule, people were able to hold who they were up against God's will and character. They faced the consequences of their sin fully aware of their role in bringing those consequences about, all excuses removed.

God's Word communicates the law to us, along with all of Jesus' commands and teaching in the New Testament.

People must know what sin is before they can avoid it and try to do better. In what way(s) was the law God gave through Moses a gift, or act of grace, to mankind?

READ ROMANS 3:19-26.

Do we have any excuse or defense for our sin after receiving the law? What position does that put us in before God (v. 19)?

Consider the gospel. What solution did God provide for our sin and
its consequences?

How did this solution demonstrate both justice (fairness) in handling sin
and mercy (kind, compassionate restraint) in dealing with someone who's
done wrong?

We must recognize our own brokenness before we can see our need for a
Savior. In what way(s) does the Bible continue to serve as God's gift to mankind?

READ ROMANS 10:17.

What role does the Bible play for people putting their faith in Jesus Christ for
salvation from sin and its consequences?

Why might a person who doesn't know Jesus resist or resent God's law?

Do the words, actions, and attitudes that you express toward God's law
reinforce their misconceptions or point others toward the truth? Explain.

Examine your heart. Do your words, attitudes, and actions toward God's law
glorify God?

What God taught me today and what I plan to do about it:

_____

THE BIBLE'S ROLE IN SANCTIFICATION

Christians are called to be sanctified, or set apart, from the world.

Positional sanctification happens when you accept God's forgiveness and give your life to Jesus Christ. The very moment you do so, God adopts you into His family, setting you apart from those who haven't accepted His forgiveness yet— you are justified and declared righteous. Your positional sanctification is a work of the Holy Spirit from beginning to end, having nothing to do with who you are or what you've done for yourself and everything to do with who Jesus is and what He's done for you.

Experiential sanctification—a life-long process that begins after positional sanctification—is the direct result of cooperating with the Holy Spirit inside you. It brings spiritual maturity that sets you apart from those who don't belong to God yet. The more intentional your effort to become like Jesus Christ through obedience to God's Word and the Holy Spirit's leading, the more extensive your experiential sanctification.

Future sanctification is the completion of your positional and experiential sanctification. The Holy Spirit will accomplish this when you are reunited with Jesus. Then, and only then, will you experience the perfection you've been striving for your whole life.

READ ROMANS 6:9-14.

What does experiential sanctification look like according to this passage?

What shift has to happen in a Christian's mind and attitude for sanctification to take place as it should?

Describe how each type of sanctification glorifies God:

Positional	Experiential	Future

READ JOHN 17:17.

This is an excerpt from the prayer Jesus prayed out loud just before His arrest.

What tool did God give us to help with sanctification?

What does the Holy Spirit do for you when you faithfully study God's Word?

What does the level of your commitment to and passion for God's Word have to do with your ability to glorify Him?

READ 1 JOHN 3:1-3.

What act of God should motivate us to pursue sanctification according to this passage?

Does the world understand this motivation? Why or why not?

What God taught me today and what I plan to do about it:

_____

_____

_____

STUDYING GOD'S WORD

As a child of God, your ability to know and please the Father is directly related to the amount of effort you put into Bible study and the intentional application of Scripture.

READ 1 PETER 2:2-3.

Describe what happened and how you felt when you became a Christian.

What did Peter say was the very first step Christians take toward spiritual growth after salvation?

What can you do to maintain the intimacy with God you experienced in that moment?

READ PSALM 1:1-6; 119:97-105.

Those who understand the role the Bible plays in their salvation and sanctification—and have experienced firsthand the feeling of closeness with God it provides—crave it. In other words, the more Bible you get, the more you want, and that's okay. Bible study is an appropriate and healthy addiction.

List the benefits those who study God's Word enjoy.

Can you relate to the craving for God's Word expressed in these Psalms? Why or why not?

What perks, or benefits, have you enjoyed when you put more effort into Bible study?

Would you describe your current desire for God's Word as a craving? Explain.

READ EPHESIANS 5:15-17.

Why is it foolish for Christians not to make a serious effort to study the Bible and understand God's will for their lives?

What reason did this passage give for "making the most of the time"? What does that have to do with your mission and ultimate purpose?

Do your Bible study habits show that you're making the most of your time? Explain.

What God taught me today and what I plan to do about it:

_____

_____

_____

_____

_____

_____

_____

OBEYING GOD'S WORD

Knowing what the Bible says is not enough—we have to obey what it says to please God and grow spiritually.

READ JAMES 1:22-25.

It's a good thing to listen to sermons, and it's a good thing to take notes over personal Bible study, but neither of these efforts do any good until we apply the truth we've gathered to our lives. If we do, we will gain a deeper understanding of who God is, who we aren't, and what needs to be done about it for God to be glorified. If we don't, we'll stay right where we are spiritually.

In what way did James say Christians sometimes deceive themselves?

Have you ever tricked yourself into thinking this way? Explain.

Considering all you've learned about God's law, what are some ways the Bible is like a mirror?

READ 1 CORINTHIANS 8:1-3.

Just as kindergarteners expect everyone to be impressed by their basic knowledge, immature Christians expect people to be impressed by their knowledge of basic spiritual truths. Those who have applied those truths, found God faithful, and discovered themselves lacking tend to brag on God, not themselves.

What do you think it means that "knowledge puffs up"?

How might being a know-it-all because of your knowledge of Scripture hinder your mission?

Can you glorify God effectively while acting like a know-it-all? Why or why not?

READ 1 JOHN 5:2-4.

Surrounded by negativity and hate, Christians sometimes struggle to think of themselves as victors, or winners, but we are. Nothing can take away what Jesus has given us: eternal life, a place in God's kingdom, and the power to affect change in others' hearts, if not their circumstances. To love God is to obey Him. To obey Him is to love others. To love others is to give them a glimpse of God through all the mess and point them to victory. This is how we win.

Why aren't God's commands burdensome to those who love Him (v. 4)?

What does your knowledge of Scripture have to do with your ability to love others as God commands?

How does obeying God's Word advance the gospel and glorify Him?

What God taught me today and what I plan to do about it:

_____

_____

_____

_____

PRESERVING GOD'S WORD

God's Word is true, powerful, and eternal. He will preserve it no matter what, but you have an important role to play in the process.

READ REVELATION 22:18-19.

The Book of the Revelation is just that, a revealing of Jesus Christ and events to come written by the apostle John. While in exile, John had a vision from Jesus that detailed more of what Jesus told the apostles during His time on earth, filled Christ-followers with hope for the future, and served as a warning to those who were still living in sin. John recorded what he saw and experienced in great detail, but we need the Holy Spirit's help to interpret and understand what he recorded.

The Bible plays a major role in God's plan to rescue sinners for His own glory, so it is important that the content and message of the Bible remain unchanged even as it is translated and paraphrased over time.

What damage could a person cause by translating or paraphrasing Scripture carelessly?

Does it make sense that God would promise such harsh punishment to those who dare to tamper with it? Why or why not?

READ 2 CORINTHIANS 10:3-5.

In this passage, Paul defended himself against people who accused him of becoming like the world. Paul explained his process for guarding his heart against worldliness. He said that he held his every thought up against the knowledge of God as found in Scripture, so he could discern which thoughts and ideas were of God and which weren't. Paul's method of comparison is also helpful in preserving the integrity of God's Word over time.

Not everything that sounds biblical actually is. Even people who mean well make mistakes. The only way to make sure you never pass along incorrect information or twist God's Word is to compare everything you hear, read, and think to what God's Word actually says and throw out everything that doesn't match up.

Examine your heart. Do you hold your (and others') thoughts and ideas up to God's Word to make sure they match up before you let them take root or pass them along? Explain.

On a scale of 1 to 10, how would you rank your current level of commitment to preserving the integrity of God's Word? Why?

How will exposing and correcting half-truths glorify God?

How will passing along the absolute truth of God's Word so others can detect half-truths for themselves advance the gospel?

What God taught me today and what I plan to do about it:

WIELDING GOD'S WORD

No weapon is as powerful as the Word of God, which is why it must be handled with care.

READ EPHESIANS 6:10-17.

Although the war for our souls was won on the cross where Jesus died, Christians battle the forces of evil daily. These forces want nothing more than to weigh us down and keep us from sharing the gospel with others.

As soldiers for the cause of Jesus Christ, Christians maintain a delicate balance. With one hand, we throw out the life raft of the gospel with kindness and compassion, and with the other hand, we fight off the enemy with determination and strength. On both fronts, the Bible is our tool. If we don't handle the Bible properly, we'll wound the ones we mean to rescue and open ourselves up to the influence of evil.

This passage refers to God's Word as the "sword of the Spirit." What have you learned about the Holy Spirit's role in God's plan to rescue the world from the consequences of sin through Jesus Christ?

What have you learned about the Holy Spirit's role in the sanctification of those who put their faith in Jesus Christ for salvation?

What role does Scripture play in the work of the Holy Spirit? What makes "sword" a good description for it?

READ HEBREWS 4:12 AND 1 TIMOTHY 1:8.

Spoken by the same God who spoke the world into existence and breathed life into us, God's Word is living and active. When used properly in cooperation with the Holy Spirit, the Bible accomplishes what nothing and no one else can.

What characteristics of the Word of God were noted in these verses?

Explain the importance of listening carefully to the Holy Spirit when engaging with and using God's Word.

Why is it so important that you let God's Word speak for itself in conversation with others?

What difference does depending on God's Word instead of your own wisdom make when processing things that happen and making decisions?

How does this affect the way you live?

What God taught me today and what I plan to do about it:

_____

_____

_____

_____

_____

REVIEW DAY

Take a deep breath and spend a few minutes looking back through the Bible study guides in this chapter. Answer the following questions:

On a scale of 1 to 10, how much effort have you put into completing your daily Bible study guides?

How much attention have you devoted to hearing God's voice? What has He said to you?

How has living intentionally for God's glory affected you so far? How has it affected those around you?

If you haven't started a *100 Days* group yet, it's never too late! See The Discipleship Group Guide on page 212 for instructions.

If you're already leading a *100 Days* group, encourage members to either continue inviting people to join your group or to start their own *100 Days* group. Lead by example and celebrate what God is doing however He chooses to do it.

PRAYER

- Thank God for His Word and for speaking to your heart.
- Thank Him for loving you and for the privilege of glorifying Him through your obedience to His Word.
- Thank Him for any results that may have come from your obedience.
- Make any commitments you need to make going forward and ask God for the desire and ability to follow through on those commitments.

CHAPTER SIX

THE CHURCH

How can I glorify God in the way I treat the church?

AS YOU GO

As you work your way through Chapter 6 of this study, you can record your questions here. Write in answers when God gives them to you.

QUESTION	ANSWER	SCRIPTURAL PROOF

CHURCH AND THE CHURCH

The global church is made up of people who put their faith in Jesus Christ for salvation and follow Him in obedience according to God's Word. The church is not an organization or a building; it is a group of people.

When a subset of the church chooses to organize itself into a functional, self-sustaining group that assembles regularly, we call that a local church.

However, being a member of a local church doesn't guarantee membership in the global church. Being the limited human beings that we are, it's impossible for any person to truly know the condition of another person's heart with 100 percent accuracy. So, it is possible for people who have never put their faith in Jesus to join local churches.

Sometimes local churches don't do a good job of explaining the difference between becoming a member of the global church by becoming a Christian and becoming a member of a local church. This makes it possible for non-Christians to operate within the structure of a local church for years—or a lifetime—believing their eternity is secure when it really isn't.

Ask the Holy Spirit to guide you as you examine your heart. Are you a part of the global church?

READ MATTHEW 16:13-18.

Jesus quizzed the disciples to see if they had figured out who He really is, and Peter passed with flying colors. Having listened closely to the Holy Spirit, Peter understood and admitted Jesus is the Messiah (or deliverer) the Jews had been waiting for. This profession of faith is the foundation upon which Jesus builds His church. Anyone who makes the same profession of faith today by the faith God alone provides becomes a part of the global church.

Where and when did you accept God's forgiveness by putting your faith in Jesus Christ and surrendering your life to follow Jesus in obedience?

When and where did you make your decision to follow Jesus public?

True faith in Jesus Christ leads to a life of obedience to Him, so only those who live a life of obedience to Christ truly belong to the global church, regardless of what they claim. Time always tells whether a person's profession of faith is sincere. Peter would later prove himself to be a faithful, obedient disciple of Jesus, validating the profession of faith made in this passage.

Jesus chose this moment to give Simon a new name: Peter, which means rock. Some people think Jesus was naming Peter as the foundation of the global church, but this is inconsistent with Jesus' narrative throughout Scripture. It's possible Jesus chose this moment to rename Peter to emphasize the gospel's power to transform. The gospel can transform those who are unstable and insufficient in and of themselves—as Peter had proven himself to be—into solid people who have the ability to make an eternal impact for God's glory.

How does cooperating and identifying with others who've made the same profession of faith in Jesus glorify God?

Why is it absolutely critical to belong to a local church that preserves the integrity of God's Word and defers to its authority in all matters?

What God taught me today and what I plan to do about it:

GOD'S FAMILY

Some people claim that every human being is a child of God, but this is simply not true. All people are God's creations, but only those who put their faith in Jesus Christ for salvation are His children.

READ JOHN 1:1-4,10-13.

Those who accept God's forgiveness for sin—made possible through Jesus Christ—and surrender their lives to follow Him in obedience become children of God from that moment on. They get to call God Father and call those who share their faith brothers and sisters. They are permanently adopted by the One who has the power to keep them forever.

Unlike some earthly fathers, God is not distant. He's closer to us than our very own thoughts, because He sent the Holy Spirit to dwell within those who are adopted.

What does it mean that those who receive Jesus are born of God?

Anyone who has trusted in Jesus as Savior is a part of God's family. Are you a part of God's family? How do you know?

In what ways will it glorify God and advance the gospel for you to live like you are a part of God's family?

READ GALATIANS 3:26-29.

God does not play favorites (Rom. 2:11). If you belong to Him, then you enjoy equal status with every other member of His family, regardless of your age, race, background, gender, socioeconomic status, and so on.

Who are some of the people listed as heirs in these verses?

Paul said that all believers are _____ in Christ Jesus. How will refusing to show favoritism glorify God and advance the gospel?

READ ROMANS 8:14-17 AND HEBREWS 2:11.

If you belong to God, you are His heir and enjoy all the rights and privileges that come with that status, including the almost unbelievable privilege of getting to call Jesus Christ your brother.

How should brothers and sisters treat one another?

Does your attitude toward your brothers and sisters in Christ glorify God? Does it help or hurt your mission? Explain.

What are some steps you can take to make sure your heart and attitude toward God's family honor God?

What God taught me today and what I plan to do about it:

_____

_____

_____

_____

_____

_____

GOD'S KINGDOM

God's kingdom is not of this world. God's kingdom is the community of those who belong to God and the glory (perfection) they'll share with Him in heaven one day. Those who put their faith in Jesus Christ for salvation are not only members of God's family, but also citizens of His kingdom.

READ MATTHEW 7:21-27.

Those who belong to the kingdom of God prove their citizenship through their actions. This passage is part Jesus' Sermon on the Mount, in which Jesus revealed the difference between true and false disciples.

What separates true disciples from false disciples?

What selfish motives might people have for performing the miracles Jesus mentioned?

Why might God allow people with such motives to go ahead and accomplish kingdom tasks (Phil. 1:15-19)?

Which demonstrates faith in the gospel of Jesus Christ: religious performance or complete obedience? Which shows that we are a part of God's kingdom? Explain.

How does the obedience demonstrated by a true disciple—a citizen of His kingdom—glorify God?

READ MATTHEW 6:9-13.

Jesus taught His disciples how to pray using a template that includes several common categories of concern for Christians. This template is often called The Lord's Prayer. As He prayed, Jesus demonstrated the proper perspective and attitude to have when talking to God.

Jesus' prayer, "Your kingdom come" (v. 10), focused on both the present and future reality of God's kingdom. This request connects directly with the next one, asking that God's will be done—being part of God's kingdom means seeking His will today and forever.

What attitude must you have to be able to pray "Your kingdom come" to God and mean it?

Where does your loyalty truly lie—with an earthly kingdom or with God's kingdom? Explain.

If someone asked you to define God's kingdom, what would you say?

The gospel is essential to building the kingdom of God, and sharing the gospel glorifies God. What are some practical steps you can take to build up God's kingdom this week?

What God taught me today and what I plan to do about it:

_____

_____

_____

_____

DAY 67

THE BRIDE OF CHRIST

Throughout the New Testament, the relationship between Jesus and the church is compared to the relationship between a husband and wife. The magnificence surrounding Jewish wedding tradition illustrates the complexities of that relationship, including its progression and culmination.

READ EPHESIANS 5:25-32.

The church (bride of Christ) is a work in progress, but Jesus still loves her. Jesus died for her, covering her sin with His blood and making her clean in the eyes of God. If perfect Jesus can love an imperfect bride so selflessly, so can we by the power of the Holy Spirit.

Describe what Jesus did when He gave Himself for the church (v. 26).

Explain the purpose behind Jesus' actions (v. 27).

Did Jesus sacrifice Himself for the church before or after she was holy and blameless in God's sight? Explain. (Hint: Read Rom. 5:8.)

What are some ways Jesus continues to care for the church?

If you are a Christian, how does it feel to know that you are part of the church Jesus loves so much?

How does Jesus see you according to this passage?

When you look at your brothers and sisters in Christ, do you see failings and fault or potential and perfection through Jesus? Explain.

How does your view of others affect the way you interact with them?

Ask the Holy Spirit to guide you as you examine your heart. Does your attitude toward others and the way you treat them show Christlikeness? Why or why not?

Does your willingness to sacrifice for your brothers and sisters hinge on their willingness to do the same for you, or do you give regardless of their ability and/or willingness to do the same for you? Explain.

List some ways you can glorify God in the way you treat the bride of Christ.

What God taught me today and what I plan to do about it:

_____

_____

_____

_____

_____

_____

_____

_____

DAY 68

THE BODY OF CHRIST

After Jesus' ascension, His followers continued the work He began during His earthly ministry. They were able to accomplish great things through the power of the Holy Spirit, just as Jesus said (John 14:12).

The Holy Spirit continues to indwell those who put their faith in Him today, unifying Christians as we work toward a common goal—the advancement of the gospel for the glory of God. Together, we form the body of Christ in His physical absence both in function and in purpose. As the body of Christ, we are bound to and dependent upon one another for spiritual growth and success in our mission.

READ 1 CORINTHIANS 12:12-27.

God put the body of Christ together Himself. Why is it so important that there be no division in the body?

What kinds of issues or events might cause division in the body of Christ?

The Holy Spirit lives inside every Christian, speaks only what He hears from God, and does not contradict Himself. What can we infer about the cause of divisions in the body of Christ?

How might divisions in the body of Christ harm its mission?

Is it always easy to remain unified with other believers? Why or why not?

What does unity in the body of Christ show? How does that glorify God?

READ COLOSSIANS 1:15-18.

The members of the Colossian church were surrounded by people who wanted them to accept doctrine contrary to the gospel of Jesus Christ and weave it into their belief system. In this letter, Paul emphasized the importance of recognizing Jesus as the head of the body of Christ (the church). Paul wanted the Colossians to hold all doctrine presented to them up to Jesus' teachings and the gospel, while tossing out everything that didn't match up.

How should Jesus' position as the head of the church affect the way we handle conflicts and divisions?

What would that require of all members involved in such a division?

On a scale of 1 to 10, how willing are you to commit to pursuing Jesus and handling conflicts in a godly way?

What can you do to increase your level of commitment? How will this glorify God?

What God taught me today and what I plan to do about it:

_____

_____

_____

_____

LOVING THE CHURCH

To love the church as Jesus loves the church is to extend unconditional mercy, grace, and forgiveness to your brothers and sisters in Christ.

READ 1 CORINTHIANS 13:4-7.

Notice that this passage doesn't contain any ifs, provisions, or outs for God's people. That's because loving others is about responding to them in a way that reflects God's character regardless of the way they've acted toward us, even when what's needed is confrontation or correction. We don't love others because we trust them; we love others because we trust God.

List the characteristics of love mentioned in this passage.

Which characteristics of love come more easily to you?

Which characteristics do you find more difficult to demonstrate?

Are some church members easier or more difficult for you to love than others? Explain.

For each characteristic listed, explain how having sincere faith in God's ability to save and transform sinners into the image of Jesus could help you demonstrate each characteristic equally to all members of the church.

Love begets love. Some people are visual learners; they don't fully understand until they see. Some people are auditory learners; they don't fully understand until they hear. Some people are tactile learners; they don't fully understand until they do with help. This being true, the best way to make a real difference in the world is to demonstrate, speak, and encourage love so others can follow our example.

Who in your church challenges you to love your brothers and sisters in Christ better?

What are some steps you can take to show love to others this week? How might this provide an example to other believers?

Does the way you love the church glorify God? Does it make the gospel appealing to those who don't know Jesus yet? Explain.

Identify some people you struggle to love well. Ask God to specifically increase your love for these people and to reveal to you ways you can show that love to them.

What God taught me today and what I plan to do about it:

HUMILITY IN THE CHURCH

Loving the church means putting the needs of your brothers and sisters in Christ above your own, just as Jesus put your needs above His when He died on the cross for your sin.

READ PHILIPPIANS 2:1-4.

What encouragement do you have from being united with Jesus Christ?

What comfort do you find in His unconditional love?

What have you experienced as a result of the Holy Spirit's presence in your life?

Sympathizing with someone means understanding what they're going through and caring about it. Empathizing with someone means hurting with them as if you're experiencing their situation yourself. Feeling compassion is wanting to do something to help others through what they are facing, even if they've brought the pain and difficulty they're experiencing upon themselves.

How did Jesus demonstrate kindness and compassion for you?

How can Christians express their gratitude for what God has done for them?

Considering others as more important (v. 3), doesn't mean you can (or should) overlook your personal concerns. Paul offered some clarity in verse 4, calling believers to look out for themselves *and* others. In other words, Christians should be responsible by looking out for what God has given them—including the brothers and sisters in Christ God has placed around them.

What did Paul instruct Christians to avoid (v. 3)? What did he tell them to do instead (v. 3)?

How will looking out for the interests of your brothers and sisters in Christ benefit the church as a whole? How will this advance the gospel?

List some ways you can glorify God as you serve your brothers and sisters in Christ.

What God taught me today and what I plan to do about it:

PARTICIPATING WITH THE CHURCH

The church is not an organization; it's a body of living members that requires the time, attention, and cooperation of its members in order to grow, thrive, and reach its goals as God intends.

READ ACTS 2:42-47.

The events described in this passage happened just after Pentecost, when the Holy Spirit came to indwell Jesus' disciples. Peter had just preached the first gospel message during Pentecost, a Jewish holiday for which Jews from all of the world had come to Jerusalem. Peter was prepared to obey Jesus' command to go and make disciples at the first given opportunity.

Peter invited people to experience salvation through faith in Jesus Christ, and thousands responded—the church experienced its first exponential growth spurt. The early church spent concentrated time together in the days following this legendary movement of God. Even after those who traveled to Jerusalem for Pentecost returned home to live out their new faith, Christians in Jerusalem continued to meet and encourage one another.

List some ways members of the early church spent their time.

What did they value? What evidence does this passage give?

How did God choose to bless them (v. 47)?

In what ways does enthusiastic participation in the life of the church glorify God?

READ HEBREWS 10:23-25.

What could have happened to the church if early Christians hadn't spent a significant amount of time together in those early days?

What might happen to the church today if Christians don't spend a significant amount of time together?

READ EPHESIANS 4:28.

What could have happened to the church if the early Christians hadn't been so generous in providing for one another's needs?

What might happen to the church today if Christians become takers instead of givers?

On a scale of 1 to 10, where would you place your current level of participation in a local church?

List ways you can participate more in both the local and global church.

What God taught me today and what I plan to do about it:

_____

_____

_____

GETTING ALONG

Jesus is the only perfect person who ever lived. Those of us who have put our faith in Him for salvation are in various stages of spiritual maturity. Some of us are further along in the process of transformation than others, but all of us are growing and changing into the image of Christ, as time and circumstances provide opportunity for growth with the Holy Spirit's help.

READ ROMANS 15:5-6.

All Christians share the common goal of pursuing Christlikeness, but God's rhythm of change is different in each Christian's life, unique circumstances, abilities, and giftedness, determining what lessons we learn and the order in which we learn them. Spiritually speaking, it's possible for you to be both ahead and behind one of your brothers or sisters in Christ, depending on the category of knowledge and experience.

There's no room for spiritual competition or comparison between members of the church. We all require patience. We all require encouragement. We all require grace.

What attitude did Jesus display toward His disciples during His earthly ministry (John 13:34-35)?

What does God give to Christians? How might those qualities help us live in harmony with each other?

Why do you think Paul felt compelled to remind Christians who were just learning to get along with one another that God gives endurance?

What is the end goal of adopting Jesus' attitude toward one another?

How might remembering this goal make it easier to get along with your brothers and sisters in Christ?

READ EPHESIANS 4:1-6.

The same Holy Spirit who guides and directs us also directs our brothers and sisters in Christ. How might this truth relieve some of our stress and concern and help us be patient with one another?

To "bear with" is not just to tolerate, but to share a person's burden at that person's pace. What do humility, gentleness, and patience have to do with a person's ability to "bear with" others?

Do you exhibit the spiritual fruit mentioned in this passage when interacting with your brothers and sisters in Christ? Explain.

What steps can you take to make sure you're showing this spiritual fruit when interacting with other Christians? How will this glorify God?

What God taught me today and what I plan to do about it:

_____

_____

_____

DISPUTABLE AND INDISPUTABLE MATTERS

DISPUTABLE MATTERS BETWEEN CHURCH MEMBERS ARE THOSE WHICH ARE NOT HANDLED EXPLICITLY IN SCRIPTURE, BUT MUST BE NAVIGATED ACCORDING TO PRINCIPLES LAID OUT IN SCRIPTURE. INDISPUTABLE MATTERS ARE THOSE SPECIFICALLY STATED AND HANDLED IN SCRIPTURE.

When discussing disputable matters, the integrity of God's Word, the gospel, and unity within the church must be preserved. We must handle these issues with prayer and Bible study and with an understanding of the possible outcomes or consequences. We should also examine our hearts, making sure our motives are pure.

READ ROMANS 14:13-23.

The specific "disputed matter[s]" (Rom. 14:1) Paul discussed in this passage was whether or not Christians should consume things they hadn't been allowed to consume before they became Christians.

Some members of the early church believed consuming those things would glorify God and advance the gospel by showing the freedom gained in Christ. Others believed consuming those things was a contradiction to the gospel because it failed to illustrate the sanctifying work of the Holy Spirit and that refusing to eat those things would bring glory to God.

Basically, both groups wanted to glorify God, and both groups believed their chosen pattern of behavior would advance the gospel best. Neither group was at fault if they truly chose their pattern of behavior for the reasons they claimed, but both were at fault in allowing their disagreement to cause division in the church.

What advice did Paul give in verses 13 and 19?

How do you determine if a matter is "disputed"?

What responsibility do Christians have toward their brothers and sisters in Christ where disputable matters are concerned?

Why is it important for Christians to take seriously the responsibility to build up others rather than causing them to stumble?

What counts as sin where disputable matters are concerned according to this passage?

READ PHILIPPIANS 3:15-16.

Paul had just finished expressing an attitude he hoped other leaders in the church would also have. Instead of pushing his point, he simply stated his case and backed off. When we don't see a specific command in Scripture, it's important to remember we all have the Holy Spirit to guide us, teach us, and convict us.

In what ways does the time, place, and manner in which you present your stance on matters give the Holy Spirit room to work?

List some ways you can make sure you're considering the needs of your brothers and sisters before your own in handling these difficult matters.

How does it glorify God when we put the needs of our brothers and sisters first?

What God taught me today and what I plan to do about it:

_____

_____

ENCOURAGING OTHERS

Although God has given Christians everything we need for life and godliness through the Holy Spirit (2 Pet. 1:3), it helps to have people who encourage and coach us as we all "run...the race that lies before us" (Heb. 12:1).

READ 1 THESSALONIANS 5:9-15.

The Christians in Thessalonica were famous for loving each other well. Even so, Paul gave these new believers more in-depth instructions for living out their faith daily.

Awake means your body and spirit are both alive, and *asleep* means your body is dead and your spirit is alive. Why did Jesus die according to this verse?

The word "therefore" (v. 11) tells us that this instruction has something to do with the truth given in the verses just before it. What does encouraging and building up brothers and sisters in Christ have to do with living the kind of life God made possible through Jesus?

List some ways Christians can enjoy the kind of life God wants us to enjoy.

What's the difference between warning people and threatening them?

REMEMBER, EXPERIENTIAL SANCTIFICATION IS A LIFE-LONG PROCESS THAT BEGINS AFTER POSITIONAL SANCTIFICATION. THROUGH THE HOLY SPIRIT'S HELP, WE CONTINUE TO GROW AND MATURE IN OUR FAITH.

READ PHILIPPIANS 3:12-14.

In this passage, Paul described the effort he was putting into his own spiritual growth through experiential sanctification. Paul understood that the perfection he would "take hold of" in eternity was made possible through Jesus Christ and that his transformation into Jesus' image would be made complete by the power of the Holy Spirit. But Paul also understood his time on earth was not to be wasted—there were things God wanted to accomplish in and through him that required his absolute, intentional cooperation.

No doubt many of those who read or listened to his letters considered Paul to be somehow beyond or above them because of his leadership position within the church. How might Paul's confessing that he'd not yet "taken hold of" perfection or spiritual maturity have encouraged those people?

In what ways do you think Paul's confession might have motivated newer Christians? What about more mature Christians?

READ HEBREWS 10:23-25.

How does the encouragement we give our brothers and sisters advance the gospel?

When those outside the church see Christians encouraging one another, what does that show them about God? How does that glorify God?

List three people you can encourage this week and tell how you intend to encourage each one.

What God taught me today and what I plan to do about it:

_____

_____

_____

TEACHING OTHERS

It's not enough to encourage your brothers and sisters in Christ to get moving. If you want to advance God's kingdom, you need to take things a step further. Keep building up others by pointing them in the right direction, teaching them the truth of God's Word, and showing them what it looks like to live out their faith.

READ 1 CORINTHIANS 10:31–11:1.

What was Paul trying to accomplish? In what ways did Paul try to accomplish this?

Christians live to please God, not man (Gal. 1:10). When Paul said that he tried "to please everyone in everything" (1 Cor. 10:31), he didn't mean we should be people pleasers. Paul wanted to encourage the church to serve for the good of the church and God's glory.

What made Paul an example worth following?

Would your brothers and sisters in Christ do well to follow your example? Why or why not?

List a few steps you can take this week to imitate Paul.

READ JOSHUA 1:6-8 AND JUDGES 2:6-12.

Joshua was one of the twelve spies Moses sent to explore the land God promised His people—the Israelites—long before Jesus was even born. After Moses passed away, Joshua led God's people into the promised land and divided the land among them according to their inheritance. Joshua's success was a direct result of the fact that he obeyed God in every detail.

What did Joshua and the rest of his generation know from personal study and through experience?

What did they fail to do before they died? (Hint: Use verse 10 as a guide.)

Put yourself in the Israelites' place for a minute. Why do you think they overlooked such an important responsibility? What was the result?

When are you tempted to keep what you've learned to yourself? List several people and share with them what you've learned this week.

READ MATTHEW 28:18-20 AND COLOSSIANS 3:16-17.

Is it enough to live out your faith in front of your brothers and sisters in Christ, and then leave them to figure out why and how you did it? What more does God expect from you?

How will your faithfulness to teach, admonish (warn or advise), and make disciples advance the gospel and glorify God?

What God taught me today and what I plan to do about it:

_____

_____

DEALING WITH FALSE TEACHERS

Not all attacks on the church come from outside the walls of church buildings. Attacks sometimes come from the inside—some people who claim to be Christians aren't. This makes it necessary for all members of the church to compare what people say to the truth of God's Word, so they can recognize false teachers in their midst. False teachers are those who twist, manipulate, add to, or take away from the truth of God's Word. They claim to represent Jesus, but they don't.

READ 2 PETER 2:9-22 AND 1 TIMOTHY 1:3-7; 6:3-5.

Scripture is truth because the God who spoke it is truth. He can produce nothing false, so what He says can be trusted. The more you study Scripture and see how everything from the beginning of the world to its end and beyond work together, the more you realize no person, with all their human limitations, could ever have made it up. No group of people could have made it up because no group of people could have agreed on that much content.

How do false teachers behave? What makes them stand out?

After reading these descriptions, you might think it would be easy to spot false teachers, but it's not. We've gotten so used to seeing people behave badly that we often don't even notice them.

READ 2 PETER 3:17-18 AND EPHESIANS 5:11.

False teachers don't have trouble finding followers, which may be why so many Christians are reluctant to identify them. No one wants to alienate people or lose friends, but keeping silent could cost the church much more.

List some ways you can respond to false teachers.

What steps can you take to avoid being misled by false teachers?

What steps can you take to help others avoid being misled by them?

In what ways might it harm your mission and the work of the gospel if false teachers recruit a following in the church?

How will standing guard against false teachers in the church glorify God?

What God taught me today and what I plan to do about it:

RESPONDING TO CHRISTIAN CELEBRITY

While it's good and right to encourage your brothers and sisters in their obedience, it's not good or right to give them credit for what God does through them or to admire them as much or more than God. Similarly, praise and recognition must never become the motivation for your own obedience to God.

READ 1 CORINTHIANS 3:2-9.

In this passage, Paul addressed the issue of Christian celebrity, or glorifying a child of God in addition to or instead of God Himself.

By the time Apollos came on the scene in the early days of the church, Paul had already been around long enough to ruffle a few feathers. Paul planted the church, and Apollos built on Paul's foundation, helping believers grow in their faith.

Eventually, some of the believers decided to declare their loyalty to Apollos, Peter, or Paul, but these ministers didn't want to be famous. They wanted God to get the credit for what He did through them, so Paul emphasized God as the One who truly grows our faith.

What's the danger of Christian celebrity to members of the church?

What's the danger of Christian celebrity to those outside the church?

Who deserves credit for any spiritual growth that happens in a person's heart? What might lead us to believe we deserve the credit instead?

What role do you typically have in growing others' faith? Are you content to play the role God assigns you in the spiritual growth of others even if no one notices? Why or why not?

READ PHILIPPIANS 1:15-18.

How should you respond when you suspect someone is preaching the gospel for the wrong reasons?

Does your current response to Christian celebrity glorify God and advance the gospel or does it hinder the work of the gospel? Explain.

What God taught me today and what I plan to do about it:

_____

_____

_____

_____

_____

_____

_____

_____

_____

_____

RESTORING OTHERS

Even with the Holy Spirit's help, living the Christian life is challenging. Because we are imperfect people, we all step out of line from time to time and make mistakes. When this happens, we need our brothers and sisters to keep us in line. It's out of love that we make the effort to help one another grow.

READ MATTHEW 18:12-14.

Jesus told this parable—known as the parable of the lost sheep—to His disciples in the middle of a message about humility and forgiveness among believers. The sheep in the parable are members of the church.

What does this passage tell you about God's love for you and your brothers and sisters in Christ?

How will chasing after others who have wandered away from the practice of their faith and/or gotten caught up in sin glorify God?

What should God's love in chasing after the one tell you about the way you should love that "one"?

READ GALATIANS 6:1-3.

With what attitude does God expect you to chase after brothers and sisters who wander?

What approach does He expect you to take when restoring them?

What do you have to be careful of when restoring others?

Examine your heart. Does the way you currently chase after and restore brothers and sisters in Christ who've wandered glorify God? Explain.

What God taught me today and what I plan to do about it:

FORGIVING OTHERS

Contrary to popular belief, forgiveness isn't about feeling "okay" toward someone who has hurt, wronged, or offended you. Forgiveness is about releasing them from the debt you believe they owe you for their behavior. It's believing and acting as if you don't require or expect anything else from them—including an apology—regardless of the way you feel on any given day.

READ PSALM 51:4.

David knew God. David loved God. David sinned against God. That's not the way it's supposed to go, but that's the way it does go for all of us sooner or later. The sin we commit not only affects us and our fellowship with God, but also those around us.

The sin David committed affected a great number of people, both those who were directly involved in his schemes and those who were watching. No doubt many of them would have argued that David had sinned against them personally, but that's not true. Sin is anything that goes against the will and nature of God. This being true, sin is ultimately committed against God.

How might remembering this truth make it easier for you to forgive your brothers and sisters in Christ?

READ MATTHEW 6:14-15 AND COLOSSIANS 3:13.

When Jesus died on the cross for your sin, He died for all your sin, past, present, and future. When you put your faith in Him for salvation, your sin was forgiven—all of it—and God no longer holds it against you. Your status as a child of God and a citizen of His kingdom is not affected by the sins you commit after becoming a Christian. However, the sins you commit after becoming a Christian do affect the level of intimacy and fellowship you're able to enjoy with your heavenly Father.

God tells us to forgive one another. When we disobey that order, we sin. Until we repent of that sin, the intimate fellowship we enjoy with the Father as a result of our obedience will be interrupted. God cannot reward disobedience.

Who is our basis for forgiveness? What reason did Matthew and Paul give for forgiving others?

How might your refusal to forgive a brother or sister in Christ hinder your mission?

What are some ways having a healthy perspective of your own sinfulness helps you forgive others?

READ ROMANS 5:8 AND EPHESIANS 4:32.

How might forgiving others before they even ask (or even if they don't ask at all) advance the gospel?

What steps can you take to prioritize your mission to spread the gospel over your own needs, wants, and perceived rights? How will this glorify God?

What God taught me today and what I plan to do about it:

_____

_____

_____

_____

_____

_____

_____

GUIDING OTHERS

Require and group of imperfect people to cooperate with each other in the pursuit of a common goal and things are going to get messy. Sometimes, the way we handle the mess provides us with more opportunity to glorify God than simply avoiding the mess in the first place. To avoid the mess, we'd have to distance ourselves from one another, and that would keep us from operating like the body of Christ we're called to be.

READ 2 CORINTHIANS 7:8-12.

Most confrontations that happen between brothers and sisters in Christ don't really need to happen. We've got a big mission to accomplish, and we're all just imperfect people doing our best to glorify a perfect God. We ought to be able to overlook most of the things our brothers and sisters do that aggravate or hurt us, forgiving them without thought or conversation so no one loses momentum in pursuit of our common goal (Prov. 19:11).

However, when a brother or sister in Christ exhibits a pattern of behavior with potential to discredit the gospel or jeopardize the mission of the church, something must be said.

In this passage, Paul responded to a change of heart shown by the Corinthian church. In another letter, he had confronted them about their behavior toward him—behavior with potential to hinder the work of the gospel—and they had repented. Although Paul hadn't enjoyed correcting his brothers and sisters in Christ, he didn't regret his actions because they freed every person involved to get back to kingdom work.

THE WORD *REPENT* MEANS TO MAKE A CHANGE, TO TURN FROM LIVING IN SIN TO LIVING COMPLETELY FOR GOD.

What should your end goal always be when approaching brothers or sisters in Christ about their behavior?

Wounds inflicted by the Holy Spirit help and lead to change, but wounds inflicted by people cripple and hinder progress. What can you do to make sure any hurt that results from a conversation between you and a brother or sister in Christ is helpful and leads to change?

READ MATTHEW 7:1-5.

What does this passage have to do with what you learned about forgiveness yesterday?

How do you know for sure whether or not you're spiritually ready to approach a brother or sister in Christ about his or her sin?

READ 2 TIMOTHY 3:16-17.

What can you use to guide you when confronting someone about sin? Why would this be a useful tool?

Examine your heart. Does the way you've been guiding your brothers and sisters in Christ glorify God?

What God taught me today and what I plan to do about it:

_____

_____

_____

_____

REBUKING OTHERS

When handled in the right way, even the most difficult conversations between brothers and sisters in Christ can benefit the church by growing everyone involved toward spiritual maturity.

READ MATTHEW 18:15-16.

This passage follows Jesus' parable of the lost sheep and should be read with the end goal of restoring a brother or sister in Christ.

What procedure must be followed when rebuking (correcting) a brother or sister whose sin against God has affected you directly?

Why should you bring along one or two witnesses if the person doesn't listen to you the first time?

What mistake do you see people often make at this stage of the process?

Why is it so important to make sure your motives are pure, that you have let the Holy Spirit search your heart and confessed your own sin, and that you are being led by the Holy Spirit before you begin this process of correction?

READ MATTHEW 18:17.

At first, this portion of Jesus' instructions sounds harsh, but it really isn't. Since these instructions are part of a bigger discussion about restoring Christians who've wandered, we can assume Jesus' goal was still restoration.

Furthermore, Jesus' behavior toward pagans and tax collectors during his ministry on earth leads us to believe that He may have been suggesting a different approach. Treating others like pagans or tax collectors means treating them like those who don't belong to God and aren't led by the Holy Spirit. Therefore, these people are unable to understand or appreciate the importance of preserving unity in the church or advancing the gospel for God's glory.

What do you know about the transforming work of the Holy Spirit that would lead you to believe that someone who doesn't respond to loving, biblical correction from the church is probably not really a Christian?

What can you expect from someone who does know Jesus? What can they expect from the church in return?

READ 2 TIMOTHY 2:23-25.

What must you avoid at all costs when attempting to correct someone whom you believe to be a brother or sister in Christ? What should you do instead?

How will following God's instructions for rebuking a brother or sister in Christ glorify Him?

How might mishandling the process hinder the work of the gospel?

What God taught me today and what I plan to do about it:

_____

_____

_____

_____

CHURCH DISCIPLINE

Although unpleasant for everyone involved, church discipline is sometimes necessary for the preservation and health of the body of Christ.

READ 1 CORINTHIANS 5:11.

Ignorance is one thing; defiance is another. The church should patiently support and teach God's Word to those who claim to be Christians and are willing to be restored through the loving care of the church. The goal is for them to truly begin a relationship with God through faith in Jesus Christ or to reestablish intimate fellowship with God through the confession of sin and repentance. If they refuse restoration, stronger measures must be taken to protect the church and the individual.

List some reasons a person claiming to be a Christian while openly embracing sin might hinder the work of the gospel.

Why might the church's quiet tolerance of such behavior hinder its mission?

READ 1 TIMOTHY 1:18-20.

Paul's words may sound harsh, but they aren't. Ultimately, Paul had the eternal good of a brother in mind. Handing people over to Satan is not the same as condemning them to hell; it's to withdraw the support and fellowship of the church from rebellious Christians until they repent. The hope is that they recognize the danger of sin and the necessity of repentance.

It's an extreme thing to do, but the potential long-term benefit outweighs the immediate pain it might cause. This step should only be taken after much prayer, at the Holy Spirit's leading, and after every attempt has been made to restore them some other way.

Why did Paul say he had handed these men over to Satan?

> SHOWING KIND, COMPASSIONATE RESTRAINT IN
> DEALING WITH SOMEONE WHO HAS DONE WRONG

How can handing a brother or sister over to Satan be an act of mercy when done in obedience to God for His purposes? How can it be an act of grace?

> TREATING EVERYONE WITH LOVE AND RESPECT,
> WHETHER THEY DESERVE IT OR NOT.

How will your willingness to do what's best for your brothers and sisters in Christ—those in rebellion and those who are hurt by it—glorify God? Explain.

READ 1 JOHN 2:19.

What can you assume about someone who leaves the fellowship of the church without reason?

What about someone who doesn't repent and rejoin the fellowship of the church in response to biblical correction/discipline?

Describe the approach you should take in trying to reach them.

What God taught me today and what I plan to do about it:

_____

_____

_____

RECEIVING CORRECTION FROM OTHERS

The way you receive correction from your brothers and sisters in Christ says just as much about your spiritual maturity level as the way you go about correcting them, if not more.

Spiritually mature Christians who are more concerned with glorifying God than preserving self are able to appreciate loving rebuke and forgive the thoughtless words of those who correct with impure motives.

CORRECTION

READ 1 CORINTHIANS 8:1-2.

Jot down the tell-tale sign of spiritual immaturity given in this passage.

What might lead immature Christians to think more of themselves than they ought?

What's the cure for pride (v. 1)?

Remembering what it means to love as Jesus loved, how do you think this works?

READ HEBREWS 12:5-13.

What encouragement do you find in this passage?

How should you respond to biblical correction, even if the person doing the correcting handles it poorly? Why?

READ PSALM 139:23-24.

What benefit do you see in approaching God with this request on a regular basis, even if none of your brothers and sisters in Christ are willing to correct you when you're wrong?

READ MATTHEW 5:21-24.

What should you do when you know you've wronged someone or they believe you've wronged them? Why?

How will maintaining a humble, correctable, teachable spirit as you live alongside your brothers and sisters in Christ glorify God and advance the gospel?

What God taught me today and what I plan to do about it:

_____

_____

_____

_____

_____

_____

_____

PRAYING FOR OTHERS

Some people view prayer as a last resort, something you do only when you've tried everything else. Others view prayer as something you do to supplement the real effort you've made. Both are wrong. Prayer is the best effort you can make to help a situation, even if you are also able to do more. When we intercede, we become a conduit of God's power in the lives of others.

PRAY FOR SOMEONE ELSE

READ 2 CORINTHIANS 1:10-11; JAMES 5:16; AND 1 JOHN 5:16-17.

Good wishes and positive thoughts accomplish nothing—they are pitiful substitutes for prayer. But the prayers of God's children have the potential to make a real difference.

Summarize Christians' needs mentioned in these passages.

Describe how these verses motivate you to live like you should and maintain a healthy level of fellowship with your brothers and sisters in Christ.

READ 1 JOHN 5:14-15.

Describe the kinds of prayers God always answers with a "yes" (v. 14).

List what God wants for those who don't belong to Him yet.

What does God want for all of your brothers and sisters in Christ?

Write out for sure what God wants for your brothers and sisters in Christ who have wandered and/or are caught up in sin.

Which specific Bible verses back up each of the truths you mentioned?

READ ROMANS 8:26-28.

Sometimes we don't know what to say when we pray, but that's okay. As long as the desire of your heart is to see God's will done, the Holy Spirit will shape your prayers.

One way to be sure you're on the right track from the start of a prayer journey is to pray specific Bible verses back to God, those that confirm, as far as you understand them, the requests you're making.

- Simply **start** with "God, your Word says," and tell Him what it says.
- **Continue** with "So I ask you to," and tell Him what you think He wants to happen according to the verse you just quoted.
- **Finish** with "May your perfect will be done in this situation, for your glory."

Praying this way will make you more watchful and aware of God's activity in the situations you're praying about. Over time, God's responses to your prayers will help you understand Him better, influence the way you pray, and help you grow into the kind of prayer warrior that moves mountains in His name.

How will interceding for your brothers and sisters in Christ glorify God?

What God taught me today and what I plan to do about it:

_____

_____

_____

GROWING GOD'S FAMILY

Someday, Jesus will return and set right everything sin has caused to go wrong. Until then, those of us who call God Father have a family to care for and a kingdom to grow with the Holy Spirit's help.

READ 2 PETER 3:3-9.

Why hasn't Jesus returned yet according to this passage?

Who qualifies for adoption into God's family?

What did God do through Jesus Christ to qualify them?

READ MATTHEW 24:36-41.

These passages were part of a private conversation Jesus had with His disciples on the Mount of Olives. The disciples were the first to know and follow Jesus, and they struggled to wrap their minds around the truth He shared with them. In this passage, Jesus discussed events in the distant future, the kingdom of God, and His eventual return after His death, resurrection, and ascension. Those of us who enjoy citizenship in God's kingdom are still waiting for Jesus' return today. His words to His disciples are His words to us.

Remembering all you've learned about God's family and kingdom, who will be taken to glory and who will be left behind when Jesus returns?

Would your friends and family be taken or left behind if Jesus returned today? Explain.

READ MATTHEW 24:45-51.

In this parable, the servants represent members of God's family, citizens of His kingdom.

How are those of us who call ourselves Christians supposed to treat one another until Jesus returns?

What will happen if we don't treat one another the way God instructs us to?

READ MATTHEW 25:14-30.

What are those of us who belong to God supposed to do with the gospel message we've been given?

List some ways you're tempted to waste the time you've been given. How does that affect the kingdom of God? What about your relationship with God?

How will making the most of the time you've been given glorify God and advance the gospel?

What God taught me today and what I plan to do about it:

REVIEW DAY

Take a deep breath and spend a few minutes looking back through the Bible study guides in this chapter. Answer the following questions:

On a scale of 1 to 10, how much effort have you put into completing your daily Bible study guides?

How much attention have you devoted to hearing God's voice? What has He said to you?

How has living intentionally for God's glory affected you so far? How has it affected those around you?

If you haven't started a *100 Days* group, it's not too late. See the Discipleship Group Guide on page 212 for instructions. If you plan to start a group at this stage, you'll need to make plans to retake The *100 Days* Challenge after you've completed this round to ensure your *100 Days* group is successful.

If you're already leading a *100 Days* group and have members at different levels of completion, it's time to consider whether or not you will stay with your group after you've completed the study. If you don't plan to continue with your group, select a dependable, established member of your group to take your place. If you can't find anyone willing to lead, you'll need to continue until everyone is finished or until you find someone willing to lead.

PRAYER

- Thank God for His Word and for speaking to your heart.
- Thank Him for loving you and for the privilege of glorifying Him through your obedience to His Word.
- Thank Him for any results that may have come from your obedience.
- Make any commitments you need to make going forward and ask God for the desire and ability to follow through on those commitments.

CHAPTER SEVEN

THOSE OUTSIDE THE CHURCH

What are some ways I can glorify God in my response to people outside the church?

AS YOU GO

As you work your way through Chapter 7 of this study, you can record your questions here. Write in the answers as God gives them to you.

QUESTION	ANSWER	SCRIPTURAL PROOF

SEEING AND RESPONDING TO THE NEEDS OF THE CROWD

The temptation for those of us who've heard the gospel and trusted in Jesus for salvation is to only enjoy fellowship with those who have done the same. Meanwhile, we pretend those still on the outside of our huddle don't exist, but they do.

READ MATTHEW 9:35-38.

In this passage, Jesus took the time not only to *look* at the crowd, but to *see* them. Jesus saw that they were "distressed and dejected" (v. 36), victims of sin and their own sinful choices.

What emotional response did the spiritual condition of the crowd stir in Jesus?

What immediate action step did this emotional response cause Jesus to take?

Where do you fit into this story? Explain.

Do you view those outside the church as villains or victims? Explain.

What is most often your emotional response to their behavior and/or circumstances?

What action step(s) would God have you take in response to the spiritual needs of those outside the church?

READ EPHESIANS 2:13 AND TITUS 3:3-7.

Where would you be if no one had ever taken the time to see you as Jesus sees you, felt compassion for you, noticed your spiritual needs, and acted in faith to meet those needs?

What good does it do you and those around you to remember who/what you were before you put your faith in Jesus and let Him rescue you from sin?

Examine your heart: Does the way you view people outside the church glorify God? Explain.

Does the way you respond to the needs of those outside the church glorify God? Explain.

What God taught me today and what I plan to do about it:

_____

_____

_____

_____

_____

MEETING THE NEEDS OF THE CROWD

The gospel of Jesus Christ is the antidote for sin and its consequences. If you belong to God, it's your job to administer the gospel. This means pouring it freely into open hearts and minds and living in such a God-honoring way that those afflicted by sin will recognize their own sickness and perhaps welcome the relief you have to offer.

READ MATTHEW 28:18-20 AND MARK 16:15.

THE STORY OF WHAT GOD DID FOR YOU

You have to start with the gospel of Jesus Christ to make disciples of Jesus Christ. If all you ever do is share your testimony, you'll leave those outside the church with the impression the gospel is for other people, not for them. So go ahead and share your testimony, but share the gospel too.

THOSE OUTSIDE THE CHURCH: THOSE WHO HAVE NOT PLACED THEIR FAITH IN JESUS FOR SALVATION

Tell the lost about sin and its consequences, God's love and provision through His perfect Son, Jesus' obedient death and miraculous resurrection, and the new life experienced by all who put their faith Jesus. Invite them to become members of God's family by confessing their sin, putting their faith in Jesus Christ for salvation, and committing their lives to follow Him in obedience. Don't just tell them about how you came to know Jesus, show them how they can do the same.

Of course, it's not always possible to get to all this in a single conversation, but that doesn't mean you shouldn't keep working at it over time. Take every opportunity God provides to share the truth of the gospel with those who need to hear it, and let the Holy Spirit take it from there.

Prayerfully consider this: Do you leave lost people with the impression that they will always be on the outside looking in, or do your words and actions assure them of God's love even for them? Explain.

READ 2 CORINTHIANS 6:1-10.

The way you live either confirms what you say you believe or contradicts it, so watch your step! Those who know you're a Christian and/or have heard you talk about the gospel's power to save and transform lives are paying close attention to see if it's true. When you obey God, you help the lost toward salvation. When you disobey, you put yourself between them and God—the very last place you want to be.

Jesus obeyed God even in His darkest hour. Should God expect any less from you? Why or why not?

List some ways Paul said for believers to behave.

In which circumstances did Paul instruct us to behave in those ways?

Why do you think living the way God wants you to when things are difficult might do more to glorify God and advance the gospel than living the way He wants you to when things are easy?

What God taught me today and what I plan to do about it:

_____

_____

_____

_____

_____

DOING YOUR JOB AND ONLY YOUR JOB

The journey to salvation through Jesus Christ is a short one for some and a long one for others. Those of us who invest in the process don't always get to see what God accomplishes through our obedience. Because of this truth and our intense desire to see people saved, the temptation to do more than God tells us to can be strong. *Resist.*

READ MATTHEW 19:16-22.

In this passage, Jesus answered the questions of a rich young ruler who wanted to be included in God's kingdom, but on his own terms. When Jesus made it clear to the young man that he had to come to God on God's terms, the young man went away sad. There were some things he just wasn't willing to do, and Jesus didn't try to stop him.

Jesus never begged people to accept His words. He let the truth speak for itself, giving the Holy Spirit room and opportunity to work. We must do the same. When you force a spiritual issue by pleading or arguing with people, you make yourself a stumbling block, turning their focus away from God to you and overstepping your privilege as Jesus' representative.

What's the danger in pressuring someone to make a decision, even if you know it's the right decision?

Does the way you present the truth of God's Word glorify God? Explain.

READ LUKE 9:1-6.

On a trial run of sorts, Jesus' disciples went out to talk to people about the kingdom of God without Him for the first time, before He was crucified. They didn't go alone, however. Jesus sent the Holy Spirit with them, and the results were miraculous.

What did Jesus tell the disciples to do when people didn't welcome them?

Is it difficult or easy for you to believe this could glorify God? Why or why not?

What are some ways working too hard to convince a lost person of the gospel's power might backfire?

READ LUKE 4:42-44.

Why didn't Jesus stay in any one town for very long according to this passage? What was He trying to accomplish?

Keeping this in mind, in what ways might the disciples have jeopardized their mission if they'd stayed where they weren't wanted?

Do your job and leave the Holy Spirit to do His when people resist the gospel. How will this glorify God?

What God taught me today and what I plan to do about it:

_____

_____

_____

HANDLING OPPOSITION

Sometimes people respond to the gospel the way we want them to, and sometimes they don't. Sometimes they lash out at the messenger. When this happens, don't take it personally. Remember, they're not rejecting you so much as they're resisting the Holy Spirit.

READ 1 PETER 3:13-17.

They may not admit it, but people who persecute Christians for their faith suffer guilt and shame for their actions. Sometimes this just gets them more stirred up, but that's okay. Every word they speak and every action they take against us serves as an opportunity for us to explain why we can endure with joy and share the gospel.

What might someone who is set against the gospel hope to accomplish by hurting someone who preaches that gospel?

Why is it so important that you respond in love when others try to hurt you, especially when they hurt you because of Jesus?

READ LUKE 23:33-34.

Soldiers crucified Jesus while two criminals watched. Jesus had every right to condemn the soldiers, but He didn't. By resisting the temptation to fight back, He demonstrated a supernatural ability to love and forgive and proved His identity as God's Son. Seeing this, one of the criminals put his faith in Jesus for salvation. The other didn't, but that was his choice. When we love those who persecute us, we prove ourselves to be God's children, identify ourselves as people with the answers others need, and encourage others to put their faith in the One who gives us the supernatural ability to love.

How does resisting the temptation to fight back when those set against the gospel hurt you glorify God?

How will forgiving those people, before they even ask, glorify God and advance the gospel?

READ 2 THESSALONIANS 1:6-10 AND MATTHEW 13:24-30.

Although these passages are meant to provide comfort to those who are being persecuted for their faith, many Christians find they actually feel sorry for their persecutors. After all, the suffering we endure here on earth is brief and temporary compared to what awaits those who never repent.

God's willingness to let you suffer for the sake of the gospel and His glory doesn't mean He doesn't love you. Which verse(s) or word(s) in these passages show His love, even in suffering?

List a few ways God is glorified when He punishes those who reject the gospel and hurt His children.

What is God proving about Himself by waiting to punish them until they've had a chance to repent of their sin?

Is there a specific situation you're facing today in which your willingness to let Him be your defender will glorify Him? Explain.

What God taught me today and what I plan to do about it:

_____

_____

_____

PROTECTING THE CHURCH

If you belong to God, you have a responsibility to protect the church from those who actively seek to destroy her—even as you endure resistance to the gospel and personal persecution with patience and grace.

READ ACTS 20:28-31.

Paul spoke these words to the leaders of the church at Ephesus when he thought he would never see them again. In a sense, these words are part of a "last words" speech. Although individual members of various local churches had treated him badly, Paul was concerned (as we all should be) about the health and future of the church—including the members who mistreated him.

What gives the church value (v. 28)? How does this fact take away any excuse you might make for not protecting her?

On a scale of 1 to 10, how passionate are you about the health and wellbeing of the church?

READ 2 JOHN 1:6-11.

| GOD BECOMING HUMAN, TAKING ON FLESH IN THE FORM OF JESUS CHRIST |

This passage is part of John's letter to a local church. There were a lot of false teachers with a lot of incorrect theology. Specifically, these people did not believe in Jesus' incarnation. John, as an apostle and leader in the early church, had a responsibility to protect the people of the church. So, he warned them about the people who would try to deceive them.

John didn't say they could not associate with these people. When he told the church not to invite deceivers into their homes, the original phrase he used is more closely translated as the idea that they shouldn't support the false teachers' ministry. It's not a bad thing to want these people to know Jesus, and John was not instructing the church otherwise. Still, church members must be cautious, not allowing themselves or others to be led astray by the false teachings.

What damage could someone set on opposing God and the gospel do to the church if given the opportunity to influence her members?

What boundaries did John set for the church when interacting with people set against God and the gospel? What about boundaries for individuals?

READ HEBREWS 6:4-8; 10:26-29.

The writer of Hebrews referred to people who had once accepted the gospel, but later decided to reject it.

What strong language did the writer use to describe how these people viewed Jesus (v. 6)?

Why would it be important to create distance between yourself and this person and between this person and the church?

How will protecting your brothers and sisters in Christ glorify God and advance the gospel?

What God taught me today and what I plan to do about it:

_____

_____

_____

PRAYING FOR THOSE OUTSIDE THE CHURCH

God's grace is immeasurable. People's behavior may make it necessary for you to hold them at arm's length for the sake of your brothers and sisters in Christ; however, that doesn't necessarily mean they're beyond reach, their eternity is set, or you're helpless to intervene.

READ EPHESIANS 6:10-12 AND 2 TIMOTHY 2:23-26.

Those of us who belong to God are engaged in a very real battle with eternal consequences, not for ourselves—our eternity in heaven is secure through Jesus Christ—but for the souls of those who don't know Him yet. What makes this battle tricky is that those we're trying to rescue often fight us the most, not understanding we have what they need.

Who is the real enemy in the battle we're fighting?

What tone and attitude should you use when talking to these people (2 Tim. 2:25)?

How do these truths affect the way you view people who are set against God and the gospel?

READ ACTS 9:1-22 AND 1 TIMOTHY 1:15-17.

When Jesus confronted and called Saul (also known as Paul) to salvation and obedience on the road to Damascus, Paul was on his way to seriously hurt the church. He planned to rip apart families, throw innocent people in jail, and maybe send others to their death. Paul was spiritually dead at that point, bound for eternal destruction, horrible, helpless, and hopeless. But Jesus skipped the middle men, appeared to Paul directly, and saved his soul for God's glory.

In what ways did Paul's salvation and transformation glorify God? What did it prove? To whom?

List some ways Paul's transformation advanced the gospel. Jot down any locations you can remember where Paul ministered on his missionary travels.

READ MATTHEW 19:24-26.

Is any sinner too far gone to be rescued by God's mercy and grace according to this passage?

God doesn't want anyone to go to hell (1 Tim. 2:3-4), and He answers prayers prayed according to His will with a "yes." What must you continue to do for the lost, even when their behavior forces you to keep them at arm's length?

Ask the Holy Spirit to guide you as you examine your heart. Does your response to those under the control of the real enemy glorify God? Explain.

What God taught me today and what I plan to do about it:

_____

_____

_____

_____

_____

DAY 93

REVIEW DAY

You're almost there! But, before you round the last curve, look back through the Bible study guides for this chapter and answer the following questions:

On a scale of 1 to 10, how much effort have you put into completing your daily Bible study guides?

How much attention have you devoted to hearing God's voice? What has He said to you?

How has living intentionally for God's glory affected you so far? How has it affected those around you?

If you haven't started a *100 Days* group, consider doing so. At this point, you'll want to wait to ask others to join you until after you've finished. That way you can take the *100 Days* Challenge again and start fresh with them. However, you can certainly go ahead and set a start date, start talking it up, invite people, and help them get their own copies of *100 Days: The Glory Experiment*!

If you're already leading a *100 Days* group and some members aren't as far along in the study as you are, let them know at your next meeting what your plans for the future are. If you don't plan to continue with them, tell them who will be leading the group. You may even want to co-lead with that person at your next meeting.

PRAYER

- Thank God for His Word and for speaking to your heart.
- Thank Him for loving you and for the privilege of glorifying Him through your obedience to His Word.
- Thank Him for any results that may have come from your obedience.
- Make any commitments you need to make going forward and ask God for the desire and ability to follow through on those commitments

CHAPTER EIGHT

THE ENEMY

How can I glorify God in my response to the enemy?

AS YOU GO

As you work your way through Chapter 8 of this study, you can record your questions here. Write in the answers when God gives them to you.

QUESTION	ANSWER	SCRIPTURAL PROOF

IDENTIFYING THE REAL ENEMY

Although stressful circumstances and limited human vision might lead us to believe otherwise, there is only one enemy to mankind. His name is Satan, and someday God will punish him as he deserves for his sin and the pain he's caused. As powerful as Satan is, those of us who belong to God are not powerless against him. On the contrary, God has given us everything we need to stand against him in victory.

READ EZEKIEL 28:11-16.

In this passage, the prophet Ezekiel compared a human ruler to Satan to help that human ruler understand the seriousness of his sin. The king's actions so closely reflected Satan's that Ezekiel accurately pinpointed who motivated the king to act.

List the descriptions of the king given in this passage.

Describe some ways this description differs from the depictions of Satan we sometimes see.

Looking at the good qualities of the king in verses 11-15, what privileges did Satan (and the king) enjoy before he sinned? What changed?

READ ISAIAH 14:13-14.

Again, a prophet—Isaiah this time—compared a human leader to Satan to point out the seriousness of the human leader's sin.

Sin is anything that goes against the will or nature of God. What was Satan's (and the king's) sin according to this passage?

READ EZEKIEL 28:16-19.

This passage both predicts the punishment coming to the king here and the punishment that did come, is coming, and will come to Satan for his sin.

What was the first stage of the king's punishment (v. 16)? What does this indicate about Satan's punishment?

Where is Satan now (v. 17)? For what purpose?

What did the king's future hold? What about Satan's (vv. 18-19)?

How did each of the king's punishments glorify God? What about Satan's punishments?

What encouragement or comfort can you take in God's authority over Satan?

Why is it important to refuse to respond to the enemy as if he were God's equal? How will this glorify God?

What God taught me today and what I plan to do about it:

_____

_____

_____

_____

THE ENEMY'S ROLE IN OUR STORY

The struggle between Satan and humankind goes all the way back to Adam and Eve. Satan was discontent to suffer alone and determined to take us with him to his eventual punishment, but God had other plans.

READ GENESIS 2:8–3:10.

Before sin entered the world, Adam and Eve lived a perfect existence in God's presence. They were surrounded by beauty and unburdened by guilt, shame, struggle, or conflict of any kind. Then Satan showed up in the form of a serpent. Familiar enough with God and His ways to know how to twist God's truth to his advantage, Satan stirred discontentment in Eve's heart and led her to question God's character. A charmer and skilled liar, he convinced Eve to do the only thing God had asked her not to do for her own good, and Adam followed after.

What kind of life would you, a loved creation of God, have enjoyed if Satan had never interfered with mankind?

READ GENESIS 3:11-15.

What judgment did God pronounce on the serpent itself? On Satan?

What about humankind?

READ GENESIS 3:16-24.

What punishments did Adam and Eve receive?

God is both holy and just. How did this punishment glorify Him?

Understand, if Adam and Eve had been allowed to stay in the garden of Eden, they might also have eaten from the tree of life. If they had, they would have spent eternity in their sinful state with no hope of ever being brought back into right relationship with God. By banishing them, God preserved that hope, demonstrating His mercy and grace. Later, He would provide for the redemption and regeneration of all mankind through Jesus Christ. This provision made it possible for those who put their faith in Jesus to be brought back into right relationship with God and enjoy His presence for all eternity.

What other examples of God's mercy and grace do you find in this passage? Why should this inspire us to glorify Him?

What does Satan tempt you to believe about the punishments God handed out after Adam and Eve sinned?

Has the enemy changed since he tempted Eve? How do you know?

How will looking through Satan's lies and believing the truth about God no matter what glorify God?

What God taught me today and what I plan to do about it:

_____

_____

_____

LIVING IN VICTORY

Things looked pretty bleak the day Adam and Eve left the garden of Eden, but our good and gracious heavenly Father was already working things together for the good of those He would call to salvation through Jesus Christ.

READ ROMANS 5:15-21.

Satan is limited because he is a created creature. He doesn't know everything God knows. Maybe he even thought he'd started a mess in the garden of Eden that God couldn't clean up. He was wrong.

How did Jesus' death glorify God? What did it prove? To whom?

What does that mean for you?

READ JOHN 12:23-31.

In this passage, Jesus discussed His impending crucifixion, an event that looked like defeat to those who witnessed or heard about it. In reality, it was the greatest victory ever won.

What did Jesus say would happen to the "ruler of this world" (v. 31)?

How did Jesus' willingness to give His life to rescue those trapped in sin glorify God?

How will your willingness to give your all in pursuit of the same goal glorify God?

READ 1 CORINTHIANS 15:50-58 AND HEBREWS 2:14-15.

Had Jesus not died for us, the only future any of us would have would be eternal death and separation from God. But Jesus died in our place and was raised from the dead, providing for our redemption from bondage to sin and fear of death.

> TO REDEEM IS TO BUY BACK. WHEN WE TALK ABOUT JESUS REDEEMING US, WE MEAN HE PAID WITH HIS LIFE TO BRING US OUT OF SLAVERY TO SIN.

Now, those of us who put our faith in Him for salvation from the consequences of sin look forward to a bright future. Our lives were transformed and made new when we put our faith in Jesus Christ for salvation, and our bodies will one day be transformed and made new, too. Incorruptible, we'll live in the fullness of God's glory forever.

What does physical death mean for those who don't put their faith in Jesus Christ for salvation? Where's the "sting" in it?

What does physical death mean for those who do put their faith in Jesus Christ for salvation?

How do victorious people behave? Do you live in the victory of Jesus' death and resurrection? Explain.

How will choosing to live in the victory that's yours through Jesus glorify God and advance the gospel?

What God taught me today and what I plan to do about it:

THE ENEMY'S GOALS

Thanks to God, Satan can't have our eternity unless we choose to give it to him by refusing the free gift of salvation God offers to us through Jesus Christ. The best Satan can do at this point is make the most of the time he's been allowed and the territory he's been assigned. He can make things difficult for those who have heaven to look forward to and take as many souls as possible with him to his eventual destruction. But his condemnation is sure.

READ JOHN 10:10.

What does Satan hope to accomplish in our lives according to this verse?

In what way is that different from what Jesus hopes to accomplish in our lives?

READ LUKE 8:11-12; JOHN 8:44; AND 2 CORINTHIANS 4:4.

These are just a few of the many Bible passages that talk about what Satan does in the lives of people who haven't put their faith in Jesus.

What does Satan hope to steal, kill, and destroy in their lives?

How have you personally seen him do this?

READ 2 CORINTHIANS 4:8-9; 11:3; AND 1 THESSALONIANS 2:18; 3:5.

These are just a few of the many Bible passages that talk about what Satan does in the lives of Christians.

What does Satan hope to steal, kill, and destroy in the lives of Christians?

Have you ever seen him do this? Explain.

READ 1 PETER 5:8.

Why is it so important for Christians to stay alert, understanding what the enemy is trying to accomplish?

What kinds of opportunities might you have to glorify God if you keep an eye out for Satan's activity in your life?

What God taught me today and what I plan to do about it:

_____

_____

_____

_____

_____

_____

_____

_____

_____

_____

_____

_____

HOW THE ENEMY OPERATES

If Satan's outsides matched his insides—if he really looked like the ugly, red, twisted cartoon depictions we see of him—maybe no one would ever fall for his evil schemes. Unfortunately, Satan is an attractive, smooth-talking charmer. Thankfully, the Holy Spirit helps Christians tell good from evil and discern Satan's activity in the world around us so we can avoid his traps and steer others clear of them, too.

READ 2 CORINTHIANS 11:14.

Describe the way Satan disguises himself.

What in Satan's background allows him to do this well?

READ MATTHEW 13:38-39; EPHESIANS 6:11-12; AND 2 TIMOTHY 2:25-26.

Satan doesn't do all of his dirty work himself. Who does he use according to these passages?

Of these three types of accomplices, which do we usually least expect? Why?

READ 1 JOHN 4:1-3.

Why is it so important to test the spirit behind people's words, actions, and attitudes?

How will only paying attention to influences that fully embrace the whole gospel and responding to it properly glorify God?

READ MATTHEW 16:21-23.

Judas Iscariot—the disciple who sold Jesus out for thirty pieces of silver—wasn't the only disciple ever used by Satan. Peter also gave way to temptation in a weak moment and became Satan's accomplice without even realizing it. It could be that Peter didn't want to lose his friend. Or maybe he was embarrassed by what Jesus—his fearless leader—was saying about His own death in front of others and wanted him to take it back. Whether selfish or prideful, Peter was still in the wrong. Jesus is always in tune with the Father and recognized Satan's scheme for what it was and resisted.

What steps can you take to make sure you don't become Satan's accomplice without realizing it?

How will checking your motives against God's Word glorify Him and advance the gospel?

What God taught me today and what I plan to do about it:

THE ENEMY'S LIMITS

Satan is persuasive and powerful and deserves our respect (Jude 1:8-10), but he's not without limits. God has seen to that. When we give Satan credit for every less than wonderful thing that happens in our lives, we glorify him instead of God.

READ JOB 1:9-22.

Nothing comes into our lives that God does not allow; to suggest otherwise is to challenge His sovereignty. Satan is responsible for some of the bad things that happen to us, but not all of them. Some are the result of sinful choices people make by the free will God gave them—the same free will that allows them to choose Him and bring Him glory in doing so. Others come with living in a broken world. Others are simply the result of living in temporary bodies subject to weakness, disease, and death. Some things we categorize as being bad only become bad when we respond to them inappropriately. When we cooperate with God, we glorify Him through our obedience. When we don't, we give Him the opportunity to demonstrate His justice, and He is still glorified.

What did Satan take from Job?

Describe Job's response and attitude (v. 22).

READ GENESIS 50:18-21.

Although Joseph had every reason to believe his life would be easy—especially after receiving a promise from God in a dream that he would one day hold a position of leadership over his brothers—it wasn't. In fact, even as he did his best to trust and obey God, Joseph's circumstances went from bad to worse. Nonetheless, Joseph didn't lose heart, but continued to do what was right. Eventually, God did put Joseph in a position of power. Joseph wasn't just over his brothers, but over all of Egypt. His position enabled him to administer God's grace to His people. Joseph was strengthened and matured by the hardships he'd endured and able to rise to the occasion with wisdom and humility.

What did Joseph understand about God's sovereignty?

How did Joseph's response to difficulty glorify God?

READ 2 CORINTHIANS 12:6-10.

Those who love God learn to value opportunities to glorify God, no matter what form those opportunities may take and even if they don't enjoy the process.

What opportunity did Paul's "thorn," whatever it was, give him?

What did Paul's response to this opportunity reveal about his heart? How did it glorify God?

READ JAMES 1:2-4.

What value does perseverance hold for those who belong to God? What opportunity does it give us?

What must a person value to find joy in all circumstances? How does this glorify God?

What God taught me today and what I plan to do about it:

_____

_____

_____

DEFEATING THE ENEMY

READ ROMANS 12:9 AND REVELATION 2:6.

To love God with passion is to hate evil with equal passion. Even so, those of us who love God and want to see His kingdom grow must be careful to separate the evil we hate from the captives we've been called to rescue.

How will hating the sin, but not the sinner, glorify God and advance the gospel?

READ JAMES 4:7.

What can Christians do to resist Satan? How does Satan respond?

READ EPHESIANS 6:10-20

What steps did Paul say to take as we prepare for battle against Satan?

READ JUDE 1:24-25.

Who deserves credit for every win you experience against Satan? How can you be sure He gets it?

What God taught me today and what I plan to do about it:

_____

_____

THE END?

Congratulations! You did it! Spend a few minutes thanking God for His faithfulness throughout this journey, the change He has brought in your life and the lives of those around you, and the privilege of glorifying Him.

Then, take a little time to think about what God has done through your obedience and surrendered heart over the past 100 days.

If you are a member of a *100 Days* group, let them know you've finished *The Glory Experiment* so they can celebrate with you! Prepare a brief testimony from your answers to the following questions to share at your next meeting.

What has God done through my obedience to His Word during this study?

How am I different than I was 100 days ago? How has my life changed?

In what ways have those around me been affected by my obedience over the course of this experiment?

What has living for God's glory alone cost me? Is God's glory worth the personal cost to me? Why or why not?

Where do you go from here? Well, you could take The Challenge all over again and see what God teaches you the second time through. You may want to try leading a group this time through with people who haven't conducted *The Glory Experiment* before. If you are already leading a group with members who haven't yet completed *The Glory Experiment*, you can continue with them or you can allow another established member of your group to lead.

Whatever you decide, choose right now to continue glorifying the Father in all things. Make a concrete plan for success and don't look back. You can start by filling in the following blanks.

I will become/remain an active member of _____
Church, using my spiritual gifts to serve, build up, and promote unity in
the body of Christ for God's glory alone.

I will read my Bible every day, think about what it says, and respond
appropriately to the Holy Spirit by obeying God's Word.

I will make a conscious effort to communicate with God through prayer,
praying about anything and everything at all times, letting the Holy Spirit
bend my will to match God's. I will trust God to say "yes" to everything I
ask that matches up with His will as I obey Him. I will begin by praying
for the following things:

_____

_____

_____

_____

_____

_____

_____

I will ask _____ to hold me accountable and
make sure I am continuing to live for God's glory alone.

Signed: _____

Date: _____

SO YOU'VE BEEN INTRODUCED TO JESUS. NOW WHAT?

If you want to put your faith in Jesus Christ for your eternal salvation, you are welcome to use the following example prayer to express that desire to God. These specific words hold no power in and of themselves. There are many ways to express these same ideas. However, if the words below accurately reflect the attitude and intentions of your heart, pray with confidence that God will wipe away your sin, change you from the inside out, and make you His child forever.

Dear God,

I know that I'm a sinner. I know my sin separates me from You and there's nothing I can do on my own to get rid of it. But I also know You love me and sent Your perfect Son, Jesus, to die in my place on the cross. Today, I put my faith in Jesus alone for my eternal salvation. Because of what He did, please wipe away my sin and make me brand new from the inside out. Thank you, Father, for adopting me into your family and calling me your child forever. Be glorified in me always!

Amen

Congratulations! If this prayer matches the attitude and intentions of your heart and you were able to pray it with absolute sincerity, you're now a child of God. The Bible says all of heaven is rejoicing over your salvation (Luke 15:10)!

Why not let your brothers and sisters here on earth celebrate, too? You have so many, and they would love to know about the miracle God just performed in you!

While the experience is still fresh, contact a couple of Christians you know and tell them what you just did so they can celebrate with you. If you're a member of a *100 Days* group, be sure to tell your group as soon as you get the chance. If you attend a local church, let your church leadership and/or your small group leader know. The more support you can get, the better!

DISCIPLESHIP GROUP GUIDE

LEADING A 100 DAYS GROUP

You can complete this experiment on your own, of course, but you may want to go on this journey with friends for encouragement and support. Use the following guidelines to lead an effective 100 Days *group.*

Invite your friends and help them get their own copies of *100 Days: The Glory Experiment*.

Model consistency in daily Bible study. You don't have to keep up with everyone in your group or finish *The Glory Experiment* ahead of your group to lead, but you do need to keep moving forward.

Set a regular time to meet that works for all group members. Don't set attendance requirements, though. Let people show up because they want to, not because they feel obligated.

Keep meetings on track without being bossy.

- Open with prayer (you or someone else).
- Use some questions from The Discussion to guide conversation.
- Make sure everyone gets a chance to talk without pressuring anyone to do so.
- Ask for prayer requests and end in prayer.

Encourage group members to keep inviting new people to join as you go. The *100 Days* group questions in The Discussion apply to all the individual study guides, so it should be easy for new people to jump in and participate at any time, no matter how far along the rest of the group may be.

Allow your *100 Days* group to grow and multiply itself. By design, a single *100 Days* group can continue to meet indefinitely under either continuing or new and changing leadership as members complete *The Glory Experiment* and retake The Challenge. Each group should form new groups as it grows and splits or as members leave to start their own *100 Days* groups with new members.

Remember, the key to viral discipleship is in resisting the urge to stifle or control the work of the Holy Spirit.

Don't try to limit the number of people who join your *100 Days* group. If it gets too big to allow for easy discussion, you can do one of two things. You can set aside time at the beginning of your meeting to socialize and then split off into small groups for discussion, or you can ask one or more of your established members to break off with part of the group and start meeting on their own to create room for growth.

When you announce a group split, explain to members that you want to reach more people. Announce the leader(s) and start dates for the new group(s). Ask group members to let you know privately which group they plan to join. Don't handle this aspect of the split during your meeting.

Whatever you do, don't assign people to groups, but allow things to evolve organically. No one likes to be sent away, and no one likes to be left out. If you don't handle a *100 Days* group split carefully, hurt feelings could undo the good that's been done.

Also, don't be offended if/when individuals leave the group to start their own group with brand new members. Give them your blessing!

If you finish before others in your group, you can either keep meeting with them until they finish *The Glory Experiment* or hand leadership over to an established group member.

If you retake The Challenge, you can either continue leading the same group or choose a new leader to take your place and start a new group of your own with people who have never taken The Challenge before.

TIPS FOR 100 DAYS GROUP LEADER SUCCESS

COMMIT. See *The Glory Experiment* through to the end, no matter what the other members of your group do, and keep inviting people to join.

BE DEPENDABLE. Show up on time every time. If a scheduling conflict comes up that can't be helped, arrange ahead of time for another group member to lead your group or to begin for you.

MANAGE WELL. Keep meetings focused and on topic. Begin and end on time. If some group members want to keep talking past the regular meeting end time, pause and give everyone else a chance to slip out. Your group may want to schedule time for snacks and/or casual conversation before or after your actual meeting to protect valuable discussion time.

STAY FOCUSED ON THE GOAL. Your job is to get everyone talking openly about what God is doing in their lives, not to get your own point across or to help your group come up with a mutual take-away.

SHARE THE SPOTLIGHT. Remember that you're not teaching, but guiding discussion. Ask questions and give others a chance to talk before you jump in with an answer. In fact, you may want to consider not answering questions if discussion is going well without your input.

USE TACT. Choose your words and tone carefully so you don't embarrass, frustrate, or anger anyone. Handle any conflict that arises privately and only with those who are directly involved.

PROTECT YOUR GROUP MEMBERS. The safer they feel, the more they will participate. Encourage group members to respect one another by keeping confidences, withholding judgment, avoiding controversy, and resisting the urge to nit pick, shame, one-up, or gossip. Group members who can't do so after being corrected privately and given a chance to do better should be asked not to return to the group so they don't hinder the work of the Holy Spirit or undermine what God is trying to do.

BE HUMBLE. Remember, no matter how long you've been a Christian or how much experience you have with church programming and Bible study, none of us are perfect. Do not judge, compete with, or try to impress your group members, but use group time to encourage and build them up.

LOVE EQUALLY. Don't show favoritism even if you know some group members better than others. Greet all visitors personally and make them feel comfortable. Encourage other group members to do the same. Use words of affirmation and encouragement as often as possible during discussion.

THE DISCUSSION

Following are discussion questions you can use to lead a *100 Days* small group. Use any or all of them in the order you think is best depending on the size of your group, who's in your group, and how much time you have. To keep your meetings from becoming too predictable, you may want to choose different questions each time you meet. You'll notice that some questions are in clusters. Ask them one at a time instead of all at once to avoid confusion.

As you lead, remember the goal is not to get through the questions you've chosen. The goal is to encourage discussion, build community, and motivate group members to see *The Glory Experiment* through to the end.

- What did you learn this week, either through Bible study or by putting what you read into practice?

- Of all the truths you learned this week, which stood out to you most? Why?

- Which of the truths you learned this week in Bible study did you have the most trouble applying to your own life? Why?

- Of all the truths you learned this week in Bible study, which was the easiest to apply to your life? Explain.

- What was the easiest thing God asked you to do this week? Did you do it? What was the result?

- Describe the most difficult thing God asked you to do this week. Did you do it? What was the result?

- Which truth from your study do you most want your loved ones to understand? Why?

- What do you think would happen if your family and friends did understand the truths you want them to know?

- What is the best way for you to share that truth with your loved ones? Friends? People you don't know?

- What did God do in your heart and/or the lives of others through your obedience this week? Share examples.

- How can you be sure God gets the glory for what He accomplished?

- Did you consciously choose to disobey God in anything this week? Why?

- How might your disobedience affect you, those around you, and/or what God is able to do in your life through this experiment? What practical steps will you take to do better next week?

- What opportunities to share the gospel came up this week as a result of your obedience to God's Word? Did you share it? What was the result?

- How are you different this week than you were last week as a result of living for God's glory alone? How have those around you been affected by this change?

- How is your life different this week than it was last week as a result of living for God's glory instead of your own? How have the lives of those around you been affected by this change?

- How would your family/community/country/world be different if every Christian in it applied the truths you learned this week to their lives?

- What do you hope to see God do in your life or the lives of your family/community/country/world in the future?

- What questions do you have about what you read in God's Word this week and/or how it applies to you?

- How can we support and encourage you in the days ahead? What do you need from us? How can we pray for you?

- What positive change do you see in the attitudes/words/actions of the members of this small group as a result of their obedience to God and/or participation in *The Glory Experiment*? Give specific examples. How does this encourage you?

> Now to him who is able to protect you from stumbling and
> to make you stand in the presence of his glory, without
> blemish and with great joy, to the only God our Savior,
> through Jesus Christ our Lord, be glory, majesty, power,
> and authority before all time, now and forever. Amen.

JUDE 1:24-25

THE TRUTH

ABOUT GOD

☐ There is only one true God. God is infinite (endless), immutable (unchanging), omnipresent (everywhere), sovereign (ruler over all), omniscient (knowing everything), and omnipotent (all-powerful).
1 Kings 8:27; 1 Chronicles 28:9; Psalm 139:7-12; Isaiah 46:9-11; Ephesians 1; Hebrews 4:13; James 1:17; Revelation 1:8

☐ God is love. He is just, gracious, merciful, truthful, and holy.
Romans 3:25-26; Ephesians 2:4,8; Hebrews 6:18; 1 John 1:5; 4:8

☐ God is the Creator, the Giver and Sustainer of life. He created mankind in His image. **Genesis 1:27; Isaiah 42:5; Acts 17:28**

> A NON-BIBLICAL WORD USED TO DESCRIBE IN SIMPLE TERMS AN ABSTRACT AND COMPREHENSIVE BIBLICAL TRUTH

☐ God the Father is part of the triune Godhead, or Trinity, sharing the deity and attributes of God with Jesus and the Holy Spirit, but differing from them in personality and function. **Matthew 28:19; John 3:16; 6:27; Acts 17:29; 2 Corinthians 13:14; Ephesians 1:3-6; 4:6; Hebrews 12:9**

☐ God the Father loves us even though we are broken, willful, rebellious people. He sent His Son, Jesus, to rescue us from the sin that has held humankind captive since Adam rebelled. **John 3:16; 8:34; Romans 3:10; 5:12**

☐ God the Father extends mercy, grace, and forgiveness to all people who trust in Jesus Christ for eternal salvation from the consequences of sin and surrender their lives to follow Him. **John 1:16-18; Ephesians 1:7; Titus 3:5**

☐ God the Father adopts as full sons and daughters those who accept Jesus Christ as their Savior and Lord. He sends the Holy Spirit to live within them so they can know for sure they belong to Him forever. **John 1:12-13; Romans 8:15-16; Galatians 4:6; Ephesians 1:14; 1 John 3:1,24**

☐ God the Father uses every situation, good and bad, for the good of His children and His ultimate glory. **Romans 8:28; Ephesians 1:11**

☐ God the Father allows His children the privilege of playing a part in His plan to rescue others still trapped by sin. **2 Corinthians 5:17-20, Jude 1:22-23**

☐ God the Father takes His children to live with Him in heaven when their bodies die. **Luke 23:42-43; John 14:2-3**

ABOUT JESUS

- [ ] Jesus has always existed. **John 1:1-3,14**
- [ ] Jesus is the Son of God the Father and part of the triune Godhead (Trinity), sharing the deity and attributes of God with God the Father and the Holy Spirit, but differing from them in personality and function. **Matthew 28:18-20; Luke 7:47-48; John 1:4,48; 5:25-27; 10:30; 14:6-7; 15:26; Romans 9:5; 2 Corinthians 13:4; Philippians 2:9-11; Colossians 1:15-20; Hebrews 13:8; 1 John 5:20**
- [ ] Jesus left the glory of heaven, took on human form, and was born to a virgin. He grew up and faced all the temptations we face so He could identify with us in our weakness, but He never sinned. **Matthew 1:18-25; John 1:14; 17:5; Hebrews 2:18; 4:14-15**
- [ ] In obedience to God the Father, Jesus died a terrible death He didn't deserve on the cross to pay the price we owed for our sin. **Mark 10:45; Philippians 2:8; Hebrews 2:14-15**
- [ ] After spending three days dead in the grave, Jesus rose again, conquering spiritual death once and for all. He made a way for sinners to be permanently reconciled to God the Father. **1 Corinthians 15:3-4; Colossians 1:21-22; Hebrews 2:14-15**

> TO BE RECONCILED MEANS TO BE BROUGHT INTO RIGHT RELATIONSHIP WITH SOMEONE.

- [ ] After His resurrection, Jesus spent 40 days on earth appearing to His disciples to encourage and instruct them. Then, He ascended into heaven to be seated at the right hand of God the Father. **John 14:28; Acts 1:8-9; Hebrews 12:1-2**
- [ ] After Jesus' ascension, God the Father sent the Holy Spirit to dwell within those who had trusted in Jesus for their eternal salvation and surrendered their lives to serve Him. He continues to do so today. **Luke 4:1; John 14:12, 15-20; Galatians 4:6-7**
- [ ] Someday, Jesus will return and set right everything sin has caused to go wrong in this world. **2 Peter 3:12-13**

ABOUT THE HOLY SPIRIT

- ☐ The Holy Spirit has always existed. **Genesis 1:2**
- ☐ The Holy Spirit is part of the triune Godhead (Trinity), sharing the deity and attributes of God with God the Father and Jesus, but differing from them in personality and function. **Genesis 1:2; Psalm 139:7; Isaiah 40:13; Matthew 28:19; Luke 1:35; 11:13; John 3:5-6; 14:16-18; 16:8; Acts 5:3-4; Romans 8:1-2,15-16,26-27; 1 Corinthians 2:10-11; 6:11; 2 Corinthians 13:13; 2 Thessalonians 2:13; 2 Peter 1:20-21; 1 John 5:6**
- ☐ Following Jesus' ascension into heaven, God sent the Holy Spirit to dwell within Christians. He continues to do so today. **Luke 4:1; John 14:12,15-20; Galatians 4:6-7**

THOSE WHO ACCEPT GOD'S FREE GIFT OF SALVATION THROUGH JESUS CHRIST AND SURRENDER THEIR LIVES TO SERVE HIM IN OBEDIENCE

- ☐ The presence of the Holy Spirit in peoples' lives proves their status as children of God and guarantees they will spend eternity with Him after their bodies die. **Galatians 4:5-6; Ephesians 1:13-14; 1 John 5:12-13**
- ☐ Among other things, the Holy Spirit performs these important functions:
  - ☐ Draws people to God. **John 6:44-45**
  - ☐ Shows people the sin in their lives. **John 16:8**
  - ☐ Helps Christians pray effective prayers. **Romans 8:26-27**
  - ☐ Helps Christians understand the Bible and apply it to their lives. **John 14:26; 16:13; 1 Corinthians 2:6-16**
  - ☐ Helps Christians discern God's will for their lives. **Isaiah 30:21; Ephesians 1:17**
  - ☐ Causes Christians to bear spiritual fruit: love, joy, peace, patience, kindness, goodness, faithfulness, gentleness, and self-control. **John 15:5; Galatians 5:22-23**
  - ☐ Equips Christians with spiritual gifts with which to serve the church. **1 Corinthians 12:4-11; Hebrews 2:4**
  - ☐ Empowers Christians to do God's will. **Ephesians 3:16**
  - ☐ Gives Christians peace, joy, and hope. **Romans 15:13**

ABOUT US

- ☐ We were created by God for His glory and fellowship with Him.
  1 Corinthians 1:9; Ephesians 1:12; Revelation 4:11
- ☐ Sin is anything that goes against God's will or nature. Through Adam's disobedience, sin became a part of the human story. As a result, we are all broken, willful, rebellious people, and we sin against God.
  Romans 3:23; 5:12
- ☐ Sin separates us from God the Father, who is perfect and cannot have fellowship with imperfection, no matter how much He loves us.
  Romans 3:23; 2 Corinthians 6:14
- ☐ On our own, we are incapable of overcoming the consequences of sin and need to be rescued. **Isaiah 64:6; Romans 5:6**
- ☐ If we put our faith in Jesus Christ for salvation and surrender our lives to follow Him in obedience, then God wipes away our sin and forgets it, makes us new, adopts us as His children, and involves us in His work here on earth. Then, when our bodies die, we get to spend eternity with Him.
  Isaiah 43:25; John 1:12; Romans 10:9-10,13; 1 Corinthians 3:9; 2 Corinthians 5:17; Philippians 3:20; 1 John 1:9
- ☐ If we refuse to accept God's forgiveness through Jesus Christ, we remain separated from God the Father and face eternity in hell.
  John 3:36; 2 Thessalonians 1:7-9

| HOLD HIS DIVINE PERFECTION UP FOR THE ADMIRATION OF OTHERS |

- ☐ Those who are truly saved glorify God through praise and worship by obeying His Word, the Bible, and by letting Him have His way in our hearts and minds by the power of the Holy Spirit. **Romans 8:14; 2 Corinthians 4:7; Philippians 2:13; 1 John 3:3**

ACKNOWLEDGMENTS

I dedicate this book to my heavenly Father, the one true God, to whom I owe and gladly offer everything I have. Be glorified!

Thank you, Todd, for always encouraging me to follow God's call on my life, no matter where it leads or what it costs us. Your faith inspires me, your enthusiastic support frees me, and your example spurs me on. Imhomm, always, my love! I simply adore you.

Thank you, Hunter and Hope, for your constant encouragement. You complete the ministry team our family has become, and your dad and I don't take your partnership in Kingdom work for granted. Keep dreaming. Keep doing. Keep living for His glory. I love and admire you both!

Momma, thank you for encouraging me to dream, always being my first reader, and instilling in me a deep love for the written word. Daddy, thank you for always telling me the truth, pressing me to express myself more clearly, and holding the Bible up as the ultimate authority in our home. I love you both!

Thank you, Regina, for always being generous with your praise, affection, and affirmation. Duncan love forever, sis!

Thank you to all my *100 Days* beta testers for giving your time and effort to this project. Devon Cooper, Cari Crittenden, Heather Davis, Jayne Dickson, Karen Duncan, Rachel Franzoni, Bobby Hamil, Jana Morgan, Cory Lynne Myers, Ashley Robison, Todd Sanders, Jalyn Setser, Ashley Smith, and Linda Teel—you were an especially big help in this process. I appreciate you!

Thank you, Beejay Morgan, for rescuing, designing, and maintaining my website. Thanks for answering my endless tech questions with an amused "hehe" instead of an exasperated, "You've got to be joking!" You're a champ!

Thank you, Nelle Swindell, for being the first and only writing group I've ever been a part of. You were a gentle critic and a true friend, and I'll miss you until I join you in heaven.

Last, but not least, thank you, Ben Trueblood, John Paul Basham, Karen Daniel, Stephanie Livengood, Morgan Hawk, and Sarah Nikolai for making the publishing stage of this process a pleasure. I'm so grateful for your shared vision and enthusiasm and am excited to see what God does with and through this project!

NOTES

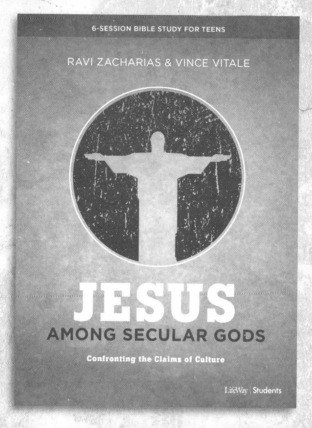